A Constitution of

Direct Democracy

Pure Democracy and the Governance
of the Future

~ Locally and Globally ~

Michael Noah Mautner, Ph.D.

Legacy Books Ltd

$$LB$$

© Copyright 1992 Michael Noah Mautner
First Edition: Legacy Books Ltd,
Second Edition: Legacy Books Ltd, 2000
P.O. Box 7465 Christchurch, New Zealand,
For more information please visit the website http://www.Legacy-Books.com
E-mail: LegacyBooks@go.com

Mautner, Michael Noah, Ph.D.
A Constitution of Direct Democracy - Pure Democracy and the Governance of the
Future ~ Locally and Globally ~

Published simultaneously on the Internet www.Legacy-Books.com

ISBN 0-473-06855-9

Table of Contents

All people share the basic needs of survival and the

social drives embedded in human nature. Survival

demands sustenance, safety and procreation; and the

social drives demand dignity, justice and freedom.

These shared values emerge when the common will is

distilled from the diverse wills of people. Where this

communal wisdom governs, human dignity will be

honored and our survival will be secure.

From the Preamble

The Constitution of Direct Democracy

Part I   The Constitution

Section 1   Preamble

All people share the basic needs of survival and the social drives basic to human nature. Survival demands sustenance, safety and procreation; and the social drives demand dignity, justice and freedom. These shared values emerge when the common will is distilled from the diverse wills of people. Therefore, where this communal wisdom governs, human dignity will be honored and our survival will be secure. Communal governance becomes vital when human decisions take control of the human future and the future of all Life. Human actions will determine if the Earth remains habitable, the level of its population, and the future expansion of Life in space. To secure this future, conflicts must be minimized to avoid self-extinction through mass weapons. Most importantly, with genetic technology the future of the essence of humanity, our communal genetic heritage, is at stake.

Such profound powers cannot be trusted to individuals with limited vision. Rather, these powers must be vested in the communal wisdom of Life that developed under the lessons of survival.

Direct Democracy is based on the decency, goodness and common sense of most people. The system also serves human dignity. In any society, individuals must subject themselves to the higher will of society. Dignity demands that this higher will shall be the common will that all formulate as equals.

Whereas the basic human needs converge, social philosophies, religions and special interests diverge and create conflicts. The proponents of social dogmas are often fanatic, and those who crave leadership are often greedy and power-hungry. Such individuals desire power most ardently and when they achieve it, they exercise power ruthlessly. The resulting tyranny often causes strife, wars and bloody revolutions, accompanied by mass suffering.

All types of democracies are preferable to such tyranny. Nevertheless, representative democracy has major intrinsic flaws. Most importantly, the system forces the irrational linkage of unrelated issues, and of issues and personalities. When an individual votes for a candidate or party, that voter necessarily promotes the *entire platform* of policies of that party, including some issues the voter may oppose. Therefore, in acting for some policies, voters are forced to act against their own principles or interests on other issues. The voter has no control over individual issues. Furthermore, politicians also yield to special interests, renege on campaign promises and surrender to corruption. Voters are also influenced by the personalities of leaders and may be swayed to vote for them despite objectionable policies.

Democracy originated with participatory citizen assemblies. The representative systems developed only to accommodate large and dispersed populations when communication technologies could not accommodate mass participation. Representatives removed from their communities had to make their own decisions, and eventually came to regard this power as a natural right.

This flawed system of government is no longer needed. Mass communication and data processing can link together populations of any size and distribution, from local to national and world governments. The public can now conduct fair and balanced debates and vote on each issue that affects them on its merits.

Fortunately, the transition to Direct Democracy needs no upheaval. It can be achieved prudently and gradually within the present systems. Through Direct Democracy Representatives who pledge to *act according to the majority will of the voters*. With Direct Democracy representatives in the majority, Parliaments or Congress will necessarily reflect the public will, issue by issue. The supporting institutions of a full Direct Democracy government, for example, the one modeled on the proposed Constitution below, can then be instituted. Of course, the system of Direct Democracy itself should be developed by communal decisions.

The principle of democratic self-government is that *decisions should be made by all members of the community, and only by members of the particular community that is affected by the decisions*. Local issues can be decidedly locally, and decisions that will affect the shared human future can be made democratically by the global human community.

The communal 'will' should be formulated jointly by all, rationally on each issue by its merits. Cumulatively, the decisions of society will control human survival and the direction of progress. These profound decisions must be based on the deepest instincts of Life that are shared by all. The common wisdom developed under the lessons of survival is the best safeguard of continuing human survival and the best guide to a limitless human future.

Life evolves, and society follows. Laws must be a solid framework for society, but not an obstacle to progress. The system must be flexible, though not fickle. Laws represent the codified will of past times, and they must be changeable. The ultimate authority must be the public will as it prevails at any time.

Section 2   Principles

1. The power to formulate laws and policies shall be vested directly in the people.

2. The people will define the major issues and policy alternatives by setting the agenda (list of issues selected for public vote) for binding referendums and polls.

3. Public decisions will be based on well-informed choice.

4. Each issue will be deliberated independently and decided strictly on its own merits.

5. Public debates will be the platform for issue discussions. People are capable of reason but are readily manipulated; therefore, public debates must be factual, balanced, impersonal and non-manipulative.

6. Public participation will be actively solicited. People exercise their power willingly, but are often inert. Public participation will be actively solicited, but not forced.

7. The results of public decisions will constitute the body of the law.

Section 3   Institutions

8. Competent Expert Agencies are accountable to the public will. They will execute public policy and ensure that the will of the people, as expressed in the referendum and poll votes, is carried out by government agencies. Expert Agencies preside over specialized areas of expertise; examples of Expert Agencies include the Health Services Expert Agency, the Defense Expert Agency, the Debates Agency and the Commerce Expert Agency.

An official elected by the public in a general election will head each Expert Agency.

9. The public will control the detailed management of the government through Policy Juries. Policy Juries are responsible for examining the actions of the Expert Agencies and ensuring that they comply with the public law. Policy Juries are non-biased bodies adjunct to each Expert Agency.

    Policy Juries will be comprised of Policy Jurors, each of whom will be trained in the specialized area of expertise of the Expert Agency to which they are attached. Membership of the Policy Juries is statistically representative of the public.

    Because Referendums and Polls can cover only major issues, the main body of detailed public law is derived from the decisions of the Policy Juries. In this sense, Policy Jury decisions play a similar role to court decisions in setting legal precedents, but they are even more authoritative as they are more representative of the public. In addition, the Policy Jury can also veto any action of the Expert Agency it finds is not adhering to the public law and requires correction.

10. There will be an elected Public Ombudsman adjunct to each Expert Agency. The Public Ombudsman will assure that the execution of policy by the Expert Agency reflects the public will.

11. Public officials must be elected strictly on the basis of competence and their attitude to towards issues. To assure this, elections will be anonymous. Professional advocates will represent the relevant merits of the candidates.

12. Checks and balances will prevail among the voting public, the Expert Agencies and the Judiciary. However, the voting public will remain the ultimate authority.

13. Public policy will be determined by annual referendum. Referendum subjects will be solicited from the public through proposals submitted to the National Proposal Bank.

14. A National Proposal Bank will sort and tally proposals submitted by the public and release them to the Debates Agency.

15. Laws and policies must be flexible but not fickle. The frequency of change will be limited.

Section 4   Principles of Competent Justice

16. A sizeable majority vote will amend the Constitution only upon a sustained demand. Constitutional amendments will be subject to repeated referendums separated by several years.

17. Laws and civil rights shall apply equally to all. Civil rights and freedoms will be guaranteed by the Constitution.

18. Fixed laws are the codified will of past populations under past circumstances. The ultimate authority must be the living will of the people as it prevails at any time.

Further Sections of the Constitution

Section 5	Procedures and Institutions	
	Article I	Public Decision Making
	Section I.1	Defining the Issues
	Section I.2	Public Debates
	Section I.3	Referendums and Polls
	Article II	Expert Management
	Section II.1	Policy Juries
	Section II.2	Expert Agencies
	Section II.3	The Executive Council and Emergency Management
	Article III	The Judiciary
	Section III.1	Expert Courts
	Section III.2	The Supreme Court and Ethics Court
	Article IV	Election and Removal of Officials
	Article V	Checks and Balances and Stability
	Article VI	Amendments to the Constitution

**Section 5 Procedures and Institutions is discussed in
Part VII Constitution (Continued)**

Organization of this book

- Discussion of the shortcoming of the representative system.

- Details of the Direct Democracy model system.

- The Direct Democracy model system will be described through some fictitious case histories.

- After the case studies the book will describe ways to change from existing representative systems to true democracy such as the model system. Various aspects and questions about Direct Democracy will also be described.

- A detailed Constitution of the Direct Democracy model and details of the various procedures and institutions are described in the last chapters of this book.

Finally, the appendix will describe the brief history of Direct Democracy campaigns and present sample campaign materials.

Part II
The Case for Direct Democracy

Chapter 1
Shortcomings of the Representative System

D emocracy is defined as "government by the people; that form of government in which the sovereign power resides in the people." The representative system fails this definition.

The main fault of the representative system is that in practice, the people cannot directly affect policies. When the public votes for politicians or parties they are actually voting for a platform with a mix of policies on various issues. This mix of issues may link together unrelated issues in arbitrary and often senseless ways.

Even when people do vote for candidates on issues, politicians and elected officials are not legally bound to their campaign platform and as a result they may reverse their stance on various issues once in office. Also, issues become linked to irrelevant personality factors. Furthermore, the representative system gives special interests disproportionate power. The outcome of these flaws is that there is often little relation between government policy and the public will. The power resides not in the people, but in a small group of elected officials and pressure groups.

These flaws originate in part when human nature itself is exposed to weaknesses of the representative system. As long as human nature does not change, true democracy can be achieved only by changing the system.

1.1 The Arbitrary Linkage of Issues

In the representative system, when you vote for a candidate you are compelled to vote for that candidate's carefully orchestrated platform of issues. There is no mechanism for individuals to vote for separate issues. This problem is intrinsic to all representative systems

7

(except through Direct Democracy Representatives as described below.)

Consider for example, the following issues: criminal penalties, abortion rights, foreign trade relations, environmental protection, disarmament, retirement benefits and race relations. Some of these are moral issues, some are primarily political or economic issues and there may be little logical interrelation among them. The policy on each separate issue should be determined on its own merits by the popular will.

In fact, most voters have a personal interest in or conviction about several of the above issues. Yet there may be no party or politician who holds the same mix of values as the particular voter. By supporting six of a candidate's ten issues, voters are compelled to vote for four issues they are opposed to. Voting for a candidate often forces most voters to compromise their own values on may issues. There is no logical necessity that this should happen.

An example of the arbitrary linkage of unrelated issues can be seen in Table 1, which shows a set of issues in the United State in 1984. Most of the same issues are still current. The majority public view can be compared in Table 1 with the national policy. The agreement of issues is no better than a random match.

Table 1 also shows the typical liberal and conservative set of views at the time and the view of two presidential candidates and several senators. The politicians mostly fall into the liberal or conservative mould. Moderate voters who hold a mix of liberal and conservative views must act against their own beliefs on half of the important issues by voting for any of the candidates.

~ Table 1 ~
Public Opinion, Government Policy, Liberal and Conservative Agendas and Presidential Candidate policy views in the United States 1984

Political Philosophy
D= Democrat, R= Republican, L= Liberal, C= Conservative

Policy	Public Opinion	National Policy	Liberal	Conserv-ative	Walter Mondale (D, L)	Ronald Reagan (R, C)
Equal Rights	Y	N	Y	N	Y	N
Abortion	Y	Y	Y	N	Y	N
Death Penalty	Y	Y	N	Y	N	Y
Gun Control	Y	N	Y	N	Y	N
School Prayer	Y	N	N	Y	N	Y
Balanced Budget	Y	N	N	Y	N	Y
National Health Insurance	Y	N	Y	N	Y	N
Nuclear Freeze	Y	N	Y	N	Y	N
Increased Defense Spending	N	Y	N	Y	N	Y
Weapons to El Salvador	N	N	N	Y	N	Y
Mining in Wilderness Areas	N	N	N	Y	N	Y
Nuclear Power Plants	Y	Y	N	Y	Y	Y

Agreement with Public Opinion (percents)						
Public Opinion	-	17	66	33	75	33
Liberal Views	66	17	-	0	91	0
Conservative Views	33	58	0	-	8	100

~ Table 2 ~
United States Senatorial Policy Views in the United States 1984

Political Philosophy
D= Democrat, R= Republican, L= Liberal, C= Conservative

Policy	Ted Kennedy (D,L)	Paul Sarbanes (D,L)	Lowell Weicker (R,L)	Mark Hatfield (R,L)	Sam Nunn (D,C)	John Warner (R,C)
Equal Rights	Y	Y	Y	Y	Y	N
Abortion	Y	Y	Y	N	N	N
Death Penalty	N	N	N	N	Y	Y
Gun Control	Y	Y	N	N	N	N
School Prayer	N	N	N	N	Y	Y
Balanced Budget	N	N	N	Y	Y	Y
National Health Insurance	Y	Y	Y	N	N	N
Nuclear Freeze	Y	Y	Y	Y	N	N
Increased Defense Spending	N	N	N	N	N	Y
Weapons to El Salvador	N	N	N	N	N	N
Mining in Wilderness Areas	N	N	N	Y	Y	Y
Nuclear Power Plants	Y	N	Y	Y	Y	Y

Agreement with Public Opinion (percents)						
Public Opinion	75	66	66	50	58	51
Liberal Views	91	100	91	50	25	8
Conservative Views	8	0	8	50	75	91

The Illogical Linkage of Issues

The problem of linking unrelated issues can be illustrated by the following examples. These are just a few of the myriad of absurdities that are caused by the representative system, which empowers one person to represent your interests on all issues.

1. The Catholic Bishops of the United States had made strong statements opposing abortion (a conservative stand) and supporting a freeze on nuclear weapons (a liberal stand). Of the six representatives in Table 2, only one adopted this combination of views. This must have caused a conflict of conscience for a Catholic voter who has strong feelings on these issues. For example, a voter who opposes abortion out of respect for all forms of life may have to vote for a conservative candidate and therefore also vote for and endorse the build-up of nuclear weapons with its risk to all forms of life. This is an obvious moral absurdity.

2. To quote another time and location, the two main parties in New Zealand in 1990 differed on their stance on retirement benefits and defense policies. A pensioner who wanted adequate retirement benefits had to also vote for military alliances with foreign nations. What logical justification is there in this linkage? After being elected, the National Party, which endorsed retirement benefits during the campaign, reneged on its promise not to apply a surtax on retirement benefits. Such betrayal of the public trust is another common shortcoming of representative governments.

3. The main parties in Israel differ on labor laws and foreign policy. A free-enterprise advocate must also vote for a militant foreign policy.
    In reality these issues have no logical connection.

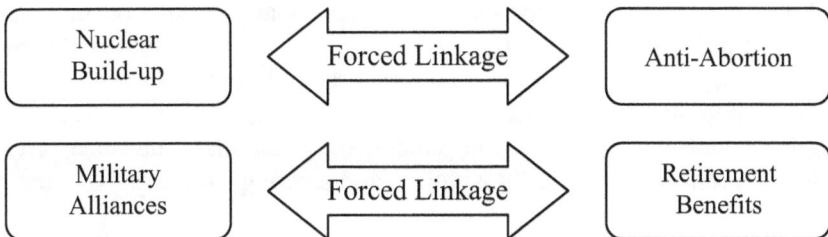

Nuclear Build-up	Forced Linkage	Anti-Abortion
Military Alliances	Forced Linkage	Retirement Benefits

4. Note that the first two examples are taken from systems with regional representation, and the third came from a proportional representative system. The very nature of the representative system links issues in such arbitrary and irrational manners regardless of their voting system.

Effects of the Linkage Problem

The linkage problem weakens the power of the public in several ways.

Diffused Public Input

Most people decide on their vote according to one or two major issues such as the economy or war-and-peace questions. When people vote for a candidate according to these issues they must compromise on secondary issues. Typical issues that are important but secondary to most voters are the environment, health care, race relations and gun control. Since these issues don't control many voters, the election often does not reflect the public opinion on these issues. Therefore the government policy on many issues, except for a few primary ones, is not directly affected by the public will.

Unpopular Policies May Long Prevail

Because of the diffused public input on secondary issues, politicians with unpopular stands on these issues can keep getting elected and unpopular policies can long prevail. The public has no recourse to reverse the policy.

Representatives Claim Public Support for Their Unpopular Views

What may appear as support for an issue, may actually be only an artefact of a different vote. Despite the fact that elections are decided on a few issues, politicians often claim that the public has endorsed *all of their views* simply by electing them. The truth is that most voters not only do not endorse all of the policies of a candidate, but also often don't even know the positions and voting records of their representatives.

Manipulation by Distraction

Governments often focus public attention on areas where they enjoy support in order to draw attention away from controversial policies. For example, governments often use or create international crises to rally patriotic fervor and to draw public attention away from economic failure. In doing so, governments deliberately use the linkage feature to gain support on account of one issue and to use this power to pursue unpopular policies in other areas.

Manipulation by Special Interests

Special interest groups can use the linkage feature to help elect favorable candidates. For example, defense contractors can finance religious populist candidates who can be elected on such emotional issues as abortion and school prayer in conservative districts. These conservative candidates often also support increased military spending. This linkage allows the defense contractors to promote their own profits by supporting religion. This again creates a morally absurd linkage between such issues as school prayer and missile programs.

1.2   Linkage of Issues and Personalities

Elections under representative democracy often focus on personalities rather than issues. With the advent of television, people often vote for a candidate on the basis of personal charisma. Great attention is paid to coaching candidates how to appear sincere, forceful and leader-like and even how to smile and use body language. The physical appearance of a candidate can swing elections. A good-looking candidate has a greater advantage, while a candidate with a disability, missing teeth or a lisp would have little chance regardless of the issues the candidates support or their

Franklin Delano Roosevelt,
U.S. President 1933 - 1945
A popular personality, popular views

abilities. All of this is of course irrelevant to the important issues that are decided by elections.

Unpopular policies can win if they are supported by charismatic personalities. An outstanding example of was the United States President Ronald Reagan. Table 1 shows that the public agreed with his stands on only 4 out of 12 important issues, while the public agreed with his opponent in the presidential race, Walter Mondale, on 9 out of the same 12 issues. Nevertheless, Ronald Reagan was elected over his opponent by a large majority and also won a second term. He enjoyed a popularity rating of over 70% by

Ronald Reagan, U.S. President Popular personality, unpopular policies.

the same public who opposed his policies on most of the prominent issues such as abortion, civil rights, tax fairness, the environment and defense spending.

Richard Nixon U.S. President 1968 - 1974 Unpopular personality, unpopular policies (Vietnam War)

Jimmy Carter, U.S. President 1976-1980 Unpopular personality, popular policies

Ronald Reagan had a reassuring, jovial, grandfatherly image and the capability of an experience actor in projecting a positive television image. The personal charisma of a retired actor helped to propagate unpopular policies in the most powerful country in the world for almost a decade.

1.3   Dealing on Issues
Wheeling and Dealing

Wheeling and dealing for votes is a common practice in Congress. For example, a Senator may gain the vote of a fellow Senator on immigration policy in exchange for supporting a space program bill that would bring contracts to the other Senator's state. By this mechanism a major space program may be decided by the pressure of immigrant farm workers. Again, this creates senseless linkages between totally unrelated issues that should be decided independently, on its own merits.

Corruption and Special Interest Groups

Politicians, especially in the United States need substantial contributions to finance the increasing pattern and need for more and more expensive election campaigns (single state senatorial campaigns often run into many tens of millions of dollars). Candidates must accept support from special interest groups to finance their campaigns. In return they are open to lobbying by these interest groups. Research by Common Cause shows strong correlations between campaign contributions and the voting records of representatives. By such means, pressure groups can achieve disproportionate power in affecting unpopular national policies. For example, the National Rifle Association has been preventing gun control legislation and the American Medical Association has been preventing national health insurance, against the public will, for decades.

Coalition Deals

In proportional representation, governments are often formed by coalitions in which minor parties often force unpopular policies on the public as a condition for supporting their major coalition partner.

1.4   A Ruling Class - The Political Elite

Once elected, representatives become members of a ruling elite. The congressional culture of lobbyists, special interest groups and large support staff, isolate representatives from the very people they were elected to represent. Although the representative is supposed to vote for and voice the interests of their voters, too often they are too distance from the people who elected them. This elitist attitude removes the public from power. Individual voters lobbying to influence representatives' votes on public policies amounts to a humiliating plea for favors, and even this right is granted most often to lobbyists with connections who have provided significant financial support.

In general, Representatives, Senators and of course Presidents are inaccessible to the individual voter. At the same time, these officials also enjoy a status of power, special privileges and sometimes profit personally from their special status.

In reality, entry into this ruling class has culturally been restricted and is much easier for rich white males than for the average citizen. For example, a large part of the United States Congress, especially Senators, are millionaires. Women and minorities are much under-represented.

Once out of office, the elected classes often move into positions as highly paid managers and political consultants; using their previous elected elitist position to further their personal fortunes. The elected ruling class hardly represents a true cross-section of the public and therefore its decisions are not necessarily faithful manifestations of the public will.

Not surprisingly, the elected ruling class refuses to share its power with the people. In most present democracies national referendums are infrequent or don't exist. At best, referendums are called at the pleasure of the ruling bodies on issues of their choosing, and offering alternative of their choice. Even so, the use of national referendums on major issues is rare.

1.5 Contradicting The Public Will

It is well known that government policy often clashes with public opinion. A concrete example is given in Table 1, which lists the prevailing United States public opinion and policy on the major issues in 1984. Only on five of the twelve issues did the national policy agree with the public. This is somewhat worse than a random fit. In other words, under this model of "government by the people", the public has as much control on public decisions as if their decisions were made by the *random flipping of a coin!*

Conclusion

Representative democracy has inherent faults that prevent the public from having true input into deciding policy. This is in the interest of politicians who hold the power and control the structure of the system.

If people want real democracy they can start by electing Direct Democracy Representatives who are committed to truly following the public will in all of their actions in Congress or Parliament. The principles of such representatives will be described in later chapters. Ultimately, the public will have to implement a system of true Direct Democracy. Most of this book will present a model system that conforms closely to the ideals of democracy. We shall also suggest ways to develop such a system from the representative system, peacefully, gradually and prudently.

Public debates will be the platform for issue discussions. People are capable of reason but are readily manipulated; therefore, public debates must be factual, balanced, impersonal and non-manipulative.

Chapter 2
The Ethical Foundations of Direct Democracy

Direct Democracy is linked to ethics, and at the deepest level, to an ethics that aims to propagate Life. This ethics will be outlined here and discussed in detail in later sections.

The Principles of Life-Centered Ethics

1. Life is a process of active self-propagation by organic molecular patterns.
2. The patterns of organic Life are embodied in biomolecules that actively reproduce through cycles of genetic information and protein action.
3. But action that leads to a selected outcome is equivalent to the pursuit of a purpose. Where there is Life there is therefore purpose.
4. The purpose of Life is self-propagation; the purpose of Life is to live.
5. Humans are part of the family of organic Life, who all share the cellular mechanisms of life and procreation.
6. Therefore, we best define our purpose by our identity as living beings. The human purpose is one with the purpose of Life.
7. Therefore the human purpose is to forever safeguard and propagate Life and to establish the living pattern as a governing force throughout the universe.
8. The human purpose defines the principles of ethics. Moral good is that which promotes Life, and evil is that which destroys Life.
9. Human actions must be governed to fulfil the human purpose.
10. This guidance is best secured by the instincts of life shared by all, that are reflected in the communal human will.

2.1 Direct Democracy and Life-Centered Ethics

The moral senses of right or wrong are basic to human nature. The desire for good to prevail motivates religion and justice, the major forces which are the basis of government and politics. Also a major motivation is a sense that we are here to serve a higher purpose, to fulfil a human destiny.

When we are proposing a new system of government, it is important to assure that it is based on proper moral foundations and at the end, satisfies our destiny. In the long term, the form of government with the most solid ethical foundations will prevail.

This ethical basis is important for even more basic reasons. At the end, our decisions, based on our ethics, will govern the direction of the human species and with it, the future of all life. The arguments for future self-governance must be therefore based on the deepest needs of our ethics and destiny.

Most people take it for granted today that democracy is the most ethical form of government, because it gives a fair say to everyone and satisfies human dignity. However, some forms of democracy do not fully satisfy these criteria. The shortcomings of the representative system were described in the preceding chapter.

The conflicts between good and evil, and the desire for dignity in the face oppression caused many conflicts throughout history. Direct Democracy can satisfy human dignity and minimize conflicts, eliminate wars and save human lives. It can also promote human rights and minimize corruption as discussed below. By these considerations, Direct Democracy is the most ethical political system.

We are currently living through times that require a profound re-examination of our ethics. Using our new technologies, future human decisions may transform humanity through genetic engineering and consequently alter the future of the Earth and all of its living species; establish our descendants throughout space, affect the future of all Life, and may even affect the fate of the universe.

All of these fateful decisions will be based on ethical judgements. To face these difficult choices, the very foundations of ethics must be re-examined. We must define good and evil and the human purpose, not as matters of abstract philosophy, but as practical guides. Our ethics must be based on the fundamental human identity as living beings and as the guardians of the future of Life. Based on these ethical definitions we must then choose a political system that is most likely to satisfy these moral principles and can also best guide us to fulfill our purpose.

In the most general sense, the insights of contemporary biology and cosmology can be synthesized into a Life-centered panbiotic ethics. This extended code of biotic ethics values the basic structures and processes that constitute Life and that are shared by all organic Life, and it encompasses both present and future Life-forms.

This ethic demands a system of government that will ultimately best serve the survival and progress of Life. These causes are best served by a communal wisdom that reflects the shared desire for safety, physical sustenance, social dignity, survival and procreation. This shared human wisdom is reflected by communal decisions that distil out the communal wisdom form the diverse drives of people.

These principles connect life-centered ethics and Direct Democracy. They may be summarized by three simple tenets.

Love Life
Respect Reality
Honor Human Dignity

2.2 The Public is Wiser than the Government - A Statistical Argument

Direct democracy is justified if the communal vote is more likely to make right decisions than a government. In this chapter we show that a majority of even mediocre voters can be make better decisions than an excellent government. The key assumption is that even marginally intelligent humans can make decisions that are at least a little better than the random flipping of a coin. It seems modest to assume that a human is smarter than a coin. Large numbers of votes will amplify even such a small advantage.

When we make decisions, some will be "right" and some will be "wrong". For the present simple model we shall assume that each decision is completely "right" or "wrong". We shall also assume that every voter has the same level of judgement, the same probability to be "right" or "wrong". More elaborate models can account for degrees of "right" or "wrong" and for people with various levels of wisdom, but the present model is enough to bring out the main point.

Given a "right" or "wrong" choice, flipping a coin would have a 50% chance of making the right choice. A human of moderate intelligence and knowledge would have a better chance to make the right choice, say 51% for a marginally intelligent person or 60% for one with some judgement. We shall call a 60% chance to be right "60% wisdom", and so on. We may also assume generously that a good government is wiser and has an 80% chance, and an excellent government has a 90% chance, to make the right choices. No reasonable leader would claim to be right 100% of the time.

The statistical argument is as follows. If any individual has more than 50% chance to make the right decision, then the more votes are cast, the higher is the chance that the majority will make the right decision. In fact, if a marginally intelligent voter has 51% chance to be right, then with a very large number of voters, it would be nearly certain that 51% of the voters would vote "right". Even this small margin would yield a majority decision that is "right". Statistically, if 100,000 of such "51% voters" do vote, then there will be a 99% chance that the majority vote would be "right". A good government with an 80% chance to be right is better than an individual with a 51% chance, but worse than the communal majority decision of 100,000 of such marginal voters. Therefore, even a marginally intelligent public would have a better chance to be wise than a good government.

Let us look at this argument more closely. If a "60% wise" person would be the only voter, there would be a 60% chance for him/her to be "right" and a 40% chance to be "wrong". If he/she voted "wrong" the decision would be wrong. In order to reach the right decision, it would be completely necessary that this one voter makes the right choice. However, if there were three voters, it would not be necessary for all of them to be right. Even if one voter is "wrong", a majority of two would be "right". With one voter there was no margin of error, while with three voters we could allow for error. With a million voters, even if 499,999 voters are "wrong", the majority decision is still "right".

For a numerical example, consider 3 voters who choose between "a" (right) with 60% chance (i.e., a probability of 0.6 to be right) and "b" (wrong) with a 40% chance (i.e., a probability of 0.4 to be wrong). The probability for all three voters to vote "a", i.e., a vote of "aaa" is $0.6 \times 0.6 \times 0.6 = 0.216$, and the probability for a vote of "aab" is $0.6 \times 0.6 \times 0.4 = 0.144$ and so on. Altogether, the vote can go aaa, aab, aba, baa, abb, bab, bba, bbb with probabilities of 0.216, 0.144, 0.144, 0.144, 0.096, 0.096, 0.096, 0.064 respectively. The first 4 combinations give a majority vote of "a" (right) (2 or 3 out of 3 votes). The sum of the probability of these first four combinations is 0.648, which is more than the 0.600 probability that one individual will vote right. As the wisdom of each voter and the number of voters increases, so does the probability that the majority will vote right. In this example, if each of the three voters has a 70% chance to vote "right" (70% wisdom), then there is already a 78.4% chance for the majority of these three voters to be right, close to the 80% wisdom of the government.

For a general analysis, we need to calculate the probability that the majority vote is "right". From the above examples, this probability increases with the probability that an individual is right, i.e., with the "wisdom" of the voters. It also increases with the number of voters. For a general case, the probability that the majority will be right can be derived from a statistical theory called Azuma's inequality, given in the Appendix. The results are presented here in a Table and as a graph. The results show, for example, that a referendum of 50,000 even just marginally intelligent "51% wise" voters has a better chance to make the right decision than an excellent "90% wise" government. With better but still mediocre "60% wise" voters, a poll of only 500 voters is wiser than an excellent "90% wise" government. Gratifyingly, the numbers are consistent with what one may expect to be a reasonable number of voters to be included in a poll or referendum.

The results of these calculations are illustrated in the figure below. The plots show the probability of a "right" majority vote as a function of the number of voters, for voters with different "degrees of wisdom". Of course, for all types of votes, the probability for the majority to be "right" increases with the number of voters. Note that the number of voters on the horizontal axis is on a logarithmic scale so that 1 on this scale means 10, 2 means 100, 3 means 1,000, 4 means 10,000 5 means 100,000 and 6 means a million voters.

In order for the majority to be wiser than the government, the plots must pass the 80% horizontal line that denotes a good government, or the 90% line that denotes an excellent government. The results show that with "51% wise" voters (the rightmost plot) about 40,000 voters are needed to produce a majority vote that exceeds a good government, and about 50,000 voters are needed to exceed an excellent government. With the somewhat better "55% wise" voters the required numbers are smaller, about 1,500 and 2,000 voters, respectively. For the better, but still mediocre "60% wise" voters, about 350 voters are needed to exceed a good and 500 votes are needed to exceed and excellent government. With the still better but realistically "65% wise" voters only about 150 are needed to exceed a good government and about 200 voters are needed to produce a majority vote that exceeds in wisdom an excellent "90% wise" government.

A reasonably intelligent and well-informed voter is likely to make the right decision at least 60% of the time, or be "60% wise" or better. Polling a few hundred of these voters will produce a majority that is more likely to be right than an "80% wise" good government or an "90% wise" excellent government. A referendum by hundreds of thousands of even less sophisticated voters will achieve the same advantage over any realistic government.

Collective Wisdom

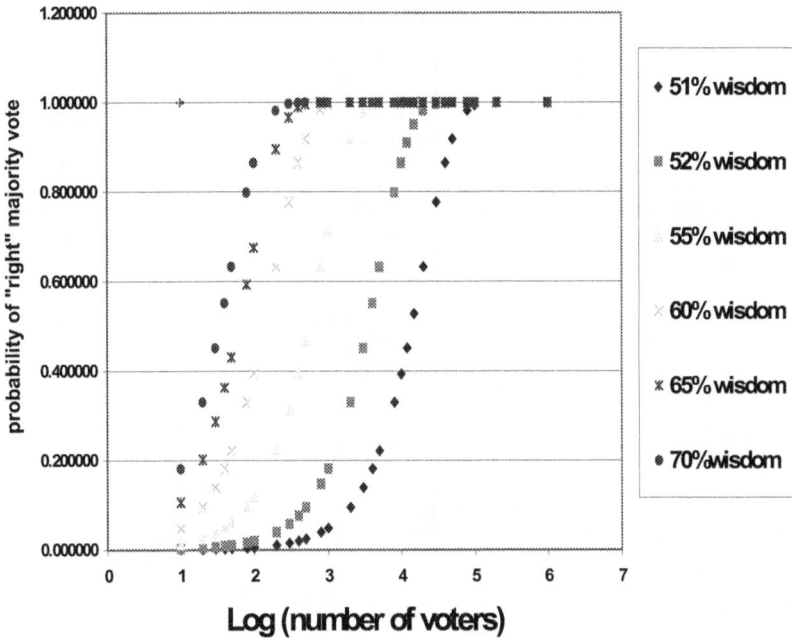

Direct democracy is justified if the communal vote is more likely to be right than the government. Statistical reasoning shows that the *majority vote is more likely to make the right choices and bring out the wisdom of the community better than any realistic government*. This is the statistical basis for the principle that the communal wisdom distils the shared values of survival, human dignity and justice from the diverse wills of people.

Institutions Of Direct Democracy

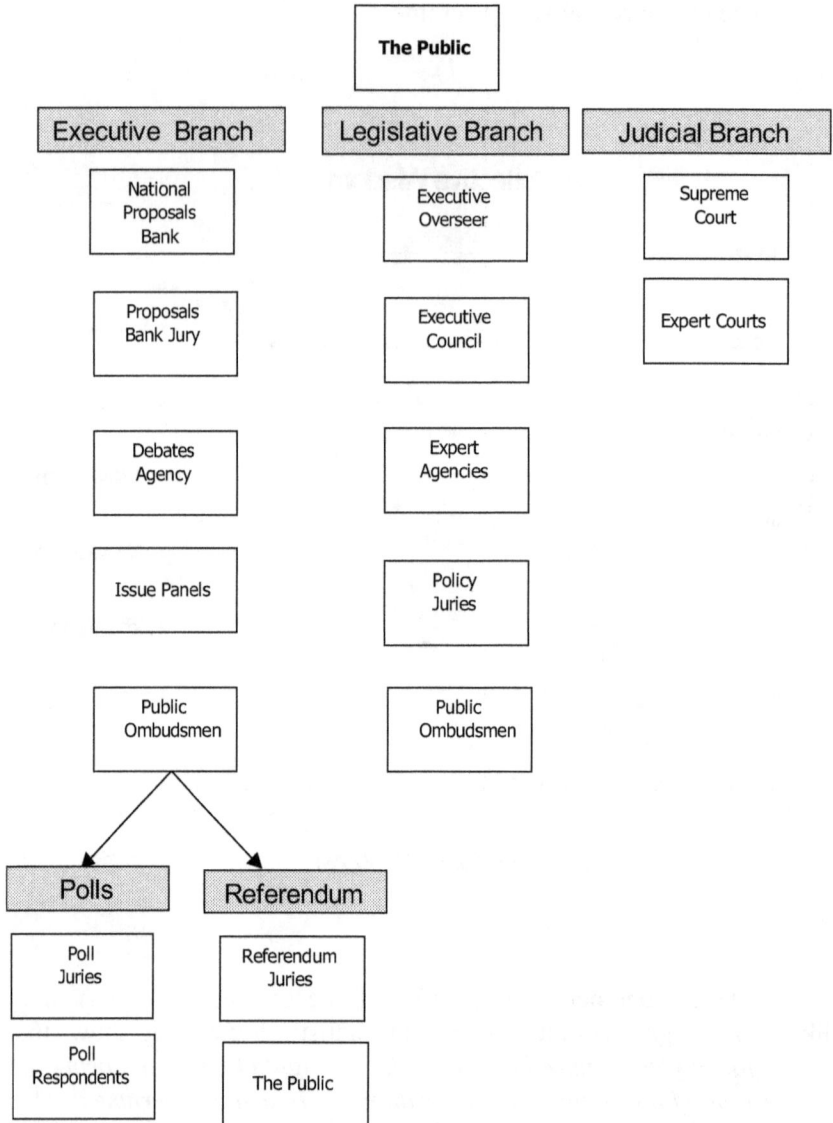

```
                          ┌─────────────────┐
                          │   The Public    │
                          └─────────────────┘

┌──────────────────┐    ┌──────────────────┐    ┌──────────────────┐
│ Executive  Branch│    │Legislative Branch│    │  Judicial Branch │
└──────────────────┘    └──────────────────┘    └──────────────────┘

   ┌───────────┐         ┌───────────┐           ┌───────────┐
   │ National  │         │ Executive │           │ Supreme   │
   │ Proposals │         │ Overseer  │           │ Court     │
   │  Bank     │         └───────────┘           └───────────┘
   └───────────┘

   ┌───────────┐         ┌───────────┐           ┌───────────┐
   │ Proposals │         │ Executive │           │Expert Courts│
   │ Bank Jury │         │ Council   │           └───────────┘
   └───────────┘         └───────────┘

   ┌───────────┐         ┌───────────┐
   │ Debates   │         │ Expert    │
   │ Agency    │         │ Agencies  │
   └───────────┘         └───────────┘

   ┌───────────┐         ┌───────────┐
   │Issue Panels│        │ Policy    │
   └───────────┘         │ Juries    │
                         └───────────┘

   ┌───────────┐         ┌───────────┐
   │ Public    │         │ Public    │
   │ Ombudsmen │         │ Ombudsmen │
   └───────────┘         └───────────┘

     ┌──────────┐   ┌──────────────┐
     │  Polls   │   │  Referendum  │
     └──────────┘   └──────────────┘

   ┌───────────┐      ┌───────────┐
   │ Poll      │      │ Referendum│
   │ Juries    │      │ Juries    │
   └───────────┘      └───────────┘

   ┌───────────┐      ┌───────────┐
   │ Poll      │      │ The Public│
   │ Respondents│     └───────────┘
   └───────────┘
```

Part III
The Model System:
Institutions and Structure

Chapter 3 Institutions of Direct Democracy:
An Overview

Step 1 - The Public Submits Proposals to the National Proposal Bank

On any level, the first public right to secure is that the policy-making agenda is itself defined by the people, through Citizen Initiated Referendums. In the proposed system this is accomplished by allowing citizens to submit referendum proposals to the National Proposal Bank. Each citizen can propose up to three issues a year.

The Referendum Process
Step 1 - The Public Submits Proposals to the National Proposal Bank

Public
Submits
Requests

Public Submission of Requests for Referendums

- Members of the public are entitled to submit three referendum proposals per year.

- The proposals are submitted to the National Proposal Bank, which then sorts and tallies the proposals into similar categories.

Step 2 - The National Proposal Bank Manages the Proposals

The proposals are sorted and tallied by the National Proposal Bank whose primary purpose is to sort the proposals into logical "issue groups". There may be thousands of similar proposals which, though worded differently, would fall into the same general category or theme. For example, there may be numerous proposals for full disarmament, others to ban all mass weapons, others to ban nuclear weapons or weapons testing, all expressed perhaps in a slightly different manner. The Proposal Bank must sort these into groups to count the proposals relating to the same issue. The adjunct Proposals Bank Jury then checks the sorting and makes decisions on proposals that are hard to categorize. Because of the large volumes involved, there may be Proposal Juries specializing in various areas such as Security and Disarmament, Human Rights, Environment, Health and so on.

Once the Proposal Bank has sorted and counted the submitted proposals, the top five issues will be subject to a Public Referendum and the next ten issues will be subject to a Public Poll. The proposals are then given to the Debates Agency to organize the debates.

The Referendum Process
Step 2 - The National Proposal Bank Manages the Proposals

The National Proposal Bank	The National Proposal Bank is responsible for: • Sorting and tallying the proposals that were submitted by the public and • releasing the issues that will proceed to the referendum and polls, to the Debates Agency.

Step 3 - The Debates

- The Debates Agency Organizes the Public Debates
- The Issue Panels Prepare the Debate Materials
- The Referendum Jury Supervises the Debates

The Debates Agency has the responsibility of organizing and conducting non-biased and informed debates. The Debates Agency forms an Issues Panel for each of the proposal issues. The task of the Issues Panel is twofold. First it ensures that the wording of the proposals retains the common content extracted from the many related proposals, and that the final wording is clear and unambiguous.

Secondly, the Issues Panels prepare the debate material.

The Referendum Process
Step 3 The Debates Agency Organizes the Public Debates

Debates Agency

Debates Agency is responsible for:

- Setting up an Issue Panel for each referendum issue (Selecting the Issue Panel coordinators and setting their schedule).
- Ensuring the debate information material is fair, clear, informative and unbiased.
- Ensuring that that information reaches the public and
- Managing the public debates on the issues.

Issue Panels

Issue Panels are responsible for:

- Formulating brief descriptions of each referendum option. These statements will then be used in public presentations and also on the referendum ballots.
- Preparing the public debate information. This includes taped debates on the subject and detailed printed and video material that would be available to all voters.

Issue Panels are composed of 10 members.

- Two representatives from the public and
- An advocate for each of the main policy options.

Referendum Juries

Referendum Juries are responsible for:

- Confirming that the list of referendum options prepared by the Issue Panels are consistent with the proposals that were originally submitted by the members of the public.
- Ensuring that the arguments for the public debate are factual and not manipulative.

Referendum Juries are composed of approximately 400 members of the public.

Information packs of debate material are then made available to the public through newspapers, magazines, television, radio, videos, movie theater advertisements, organized public debates and the ubiquitous internet. There is hardly a place that is isolated from mass communications and its reach will keep broadening. During the Debate Period, the public (for polls, the Poll Respondents) can get additional information from representatives of the Debates Agency and from volunteers and organizations knowledgeable about the issue. Throughout this period, the Referendum Jury supervises the Debates to ensure they are conducted in a balanced and non-manipulative manner.

Step 4 - The Vote
- Referendums and
- Polls

The Referendum and Polls Agency conducts the actual voting and ensures that it is available everywhere. As much as possible, voting is done through telephone banks and the internet. Voting centers may be established nationwide thereby ensuring voting access to all. Voting is done over a period of one month so that all citizens have an opportunity to cast their votes. The results are not disclosed until the end of the voting period. This prevents intermediate results from influencing outstanding votes.

Voting in a poll is done by a group of Poll Respondents who are randomly selected from the public. The number of respondents must be large enough to represent the overall voting public. For example, there may be 2,000 respondents for each poll.

Poll Issue Panels and Poll Juries supervise the selection of Poll Respondents to ensure it is random and unbiased. The tasks of the Poll Issue Panels are similar to those performed by the Issue Panels in preparing for a referendum. They have to identify the issue alternatives and prepare the issue information packs.

Step 5 - Implementation of Policy: The Expert Agencies
- Policy Juries and Public Ombudsmen Monitor the Actions of the Expert Agencies

Expert Agencies are administrative departments entrusted with the responsibility of implementing the will of the community that was previously decided through referendums and polls. Examples of Expert Agencies are the Health Services Expert Agency, the Defense Expert Agency, the Debates Agency and the Commerce Expert Agency.

Adjunct to each of these agencies are Policy Juries whose members are chosen randomly from the general population. The role of the Policy Jury is to ensure that the actions of the Expert Agencies directly reflect the will of the people. Policy Jurors receive specialized instruction in the Expert Agency's field of activities, e.g. health, employment, education etc. In order that the juries adequately represent public opinion, the size of each Policy Jury is large enough to statistically reflect the overall size of the population. For example, a Policy Jury may have 400 members who are chosen randomly from the public.

The Referendum Process

Step 5 Policy Juries and Policy Ombudsmen Oversee the Work of the Expert Agencies

Policy Juries

Policy Juries

- Are non-biased groups of citizens adjunct to each Expert Agency who are chosen at random and are statistically representative of the public at large.
- Are responsible for ensuring that the work of the Expert Agencies follows the public will and public policy.
- Give policy direction to the Expert Agency in cases where there are no existing laws about a subject. The decisions may direct the Agency how to act, or direct the Agency to request a Poll or Referendum.
- Monitor the actions of the Expert Agency and decide when the actions of the Agency conflict with the policies determined by the public.
- Have veto power over the Expert Agency with which they are associated.
- Resolve disputes between the Public Ombudsman and the Expert Agency.

Public Ombudsman	The Public Ombudsman
	• There is one Public Ombudsman associated with each Expert Agency.
	• The Public Ombudsman is responsible for ensuring that the laws enacted through public referendum and polls are upheld.

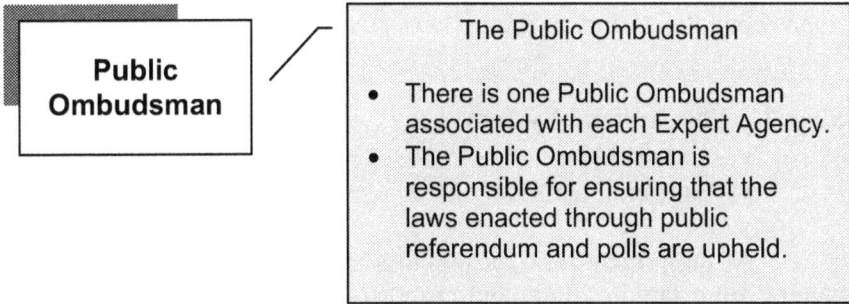

Because Referendums and Polls can cover only major issues, the main body of detailed public law is derived from the decisions of Policy Juries. If the Expert Agencies are unsure of the application of the public law, or no pertinent law exists, the Policy Juries can formulate the law. The Policy Juries have this authority, as they are representative of the public. The Policy Juries can also veto any action of the Expert Agencies they find is not adhering to the public law, and require correction.

Policy Juries meet periodically by teleconferencing. Internet chat rooms are a current development in this direction.

In addition to Policy Juries, a Public Ombudsman is attached to each Expert Agency. The role of the Public Ombudsman is to ensure that Agencies act according to the established public will. Ombudsmen also arbitrate disputes between the Expert Agencies and their associated Policy Juries and may suggest corrective actions when they find that the Expert Agency or the Policy Jury is in conflict with the public will. However, Public Ombudsmen cannot formulate new policies and cannot enforce any decisions.

Public Ombudsmen also monitor the referendum and polls processes to ensure that the debate material is fair and unbiased and is available to all citizens.

Step 6   The Executive Council Handles Emergencies that Require Immediate Attention

Situations may arise which require immediate attention. The Executive Council, which is made up of the heads of the Expert Agencies, is empowered to make decisions without the benefit of a national referendum or poll. The Executive Council must transfer the authority to handle emergency matters to the appropriate Expert Agency and Policy Jury as promptly as possible.

Step 7   The Judicial System
- Expert Courts
- Supreme Courts

At the present time most courts and judges may handle cases ranging from family affairs and criminal law to citizenship, banking, environmental issues, industrial patents, copyrights, computer fraud etc. Clearly, it is beyond the ability of any one individual to make knowledgeable judgements in all of these areas. These shortcomings become acute when the field is highly technical and requires specialized knowledge. Under Direct Democracy each Expert Court is headed by a Justice who is an established *expert* in the court's area of specialization. Justices of the courts are elected publicly.

Decisions of the Expert Courts can be appealed to the Supreme Court. The Supreme Court is composed of emeritus Expert Justices and emeritus Chiefs of Expert Agencies and the Chief Justices of the Expert Courts. When needed, these members are constituted into Expert Panels to deal with issues that require specialized knowledge. Decisions of the Supreme Court can be appealed through proposals for referendums and polls to the ultimate authority, the voting public.

• Dispute Resolution

Public policies, (i.e., laws) under Direct Democracy are determined by national referendums and polls. Expert Agencies implement those policies and Policy Juries and Public Ombudsmen monitor the Expert Agencies. When the interpretation and/or implementation of those policies are challenged, there is a formal procedure to resolve the disputes, see the following Policy Disputes Resolution Table.

Policy Disputes Resolution Table

Policy Disputes Between	Are Resolved by	Decisions Can Be Appealed to	Final Appeal
Expert Agency and Policy Jury	Public Ombudsman	Expert Court	Supreme Court can choose 1. To hear the appeal or 2. To refer to a Referendum or Poll
Two Expert Agencies	The Joint Policy Jury from each Agency	Supreme Court which can choose: 1. To hear the appeal or 2. To refer to one of the Expert Courts	Referendum and Polls
Expert Agency and Public Ombudsman	Policy Jury	Expert Court	Supreme Court can choose 1. To hear the appeal or 2. To refer to a Referendum or Poll
Public Ombudsman and Policy Jury	Expert Courts	Supreme Court	Referendum or Poll
The Public and the Expert Agency	Policy Jury	Expert Court	Supreme Court can choose 1. To hear the appeal or 2. To refer to a Referendum or Poll

The Referendum Process

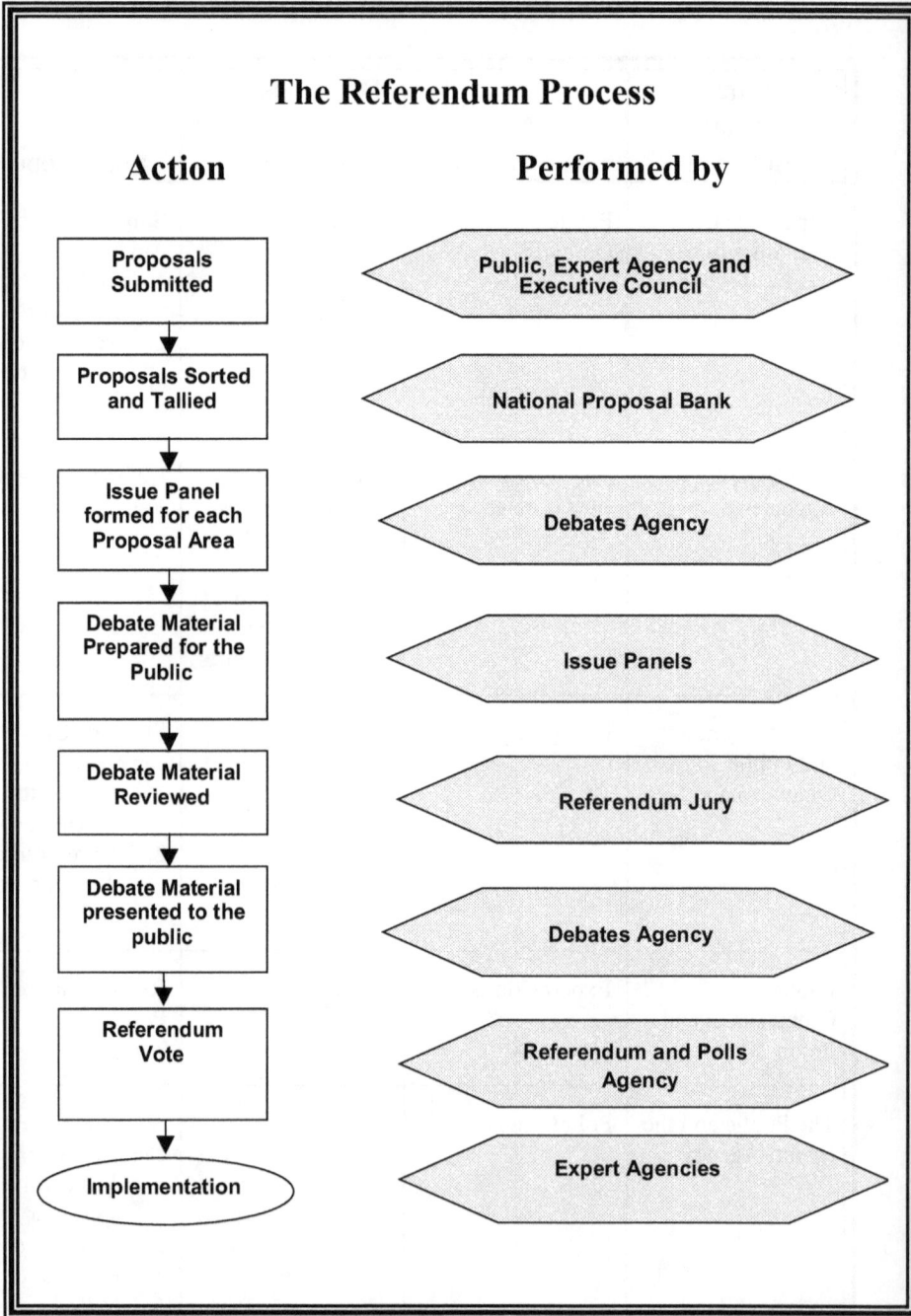

Action

Proposals Submitted

↓

Proposals Sorted and Tallied

↓

Issue Panel formed for each Proposal Area

↓

Debate Material Prepared for the Public

↓

Debate Material Reviewed

↓

Debate Material presented to the public

↓

Referendum Vote

↓

Implementation

Performed by

Public, Expert Agency and Executive Council

National Proposal Bank

Debates Agency

Issue Panels

Referendum Jury

Debates Agency

Referendum and Polls Agency

Expert Agencies

Chapter 4
Details of the Model System

No modern nation is currently governed by Direct Democracy. Therefore, a model system must first be constructed from principles. The model system described here is an ultimate objective and presents one way to implement the general principles. The same principles may be implemented through different institutions. In fact, the spirit of democracy demands that the system itself should develop under the direction of the public will and practical experience.

4.1 An Overview of Principles and Institutions

The following is a brief summary of the principles that the system must implement.

- The ultimate authority is the collective will of the people.
- The body of the law is the collection of public decisions.
- Each law and issue is decided on its merits.
- Public decision-making is based on informed and objective debates. Biased manipulation of public opinion must be prevented, and the irrelevant effects of personalities on issues should be minimized.
- The system must ensure that the ultimate authority shall be *the will of the people.* Accomplishing this is difficult because managing society requires that thousands of decisions are made daily. Therefore, a variety of levels and means for public input will be necessary.
- Public referendums and polls are the most direct means for wide-based public input. Since these can be conducted only in limited numbers, they should be reserved for major issues. Ultimately, a body of publicly enacted law will emerge, covering all aspects of legislation.
- Public input is enhanced by the input from the Policy Juries, Public Ombudsmen and the public election of senior officials.

- Publicly decided policy is implemented by Expert Agencies. The role of these bodies is one of execution and management and not one of policy or decision-making.
- Expert Agencies are guided and aided by Policy Juries that are attached to each Expert Agency. The role of Policy Juries is to monitor the actions of the Expert Agencies and intervene when these actions conflict with the policies determined by the public. These conflicts are identified by the Public Ombudsman, the Expert Court or by 20% or more of the Policy Jury members. The Agency itself may also ask for guidance from the Policy Jury.
- Policy Juries are public panels and committees that are large enough to represent a true cross-section of the overall public. Members are randomly selected from the public and are educated in the specialized fields of the Expert Agency to which they are associated. Members serve long enough to assure that the majority of the Policy Jury at any time is well versed in the field of expertise. In this way, Policy Juries combine public input with specialist expertise.
- Expert Agencies are supervised by Public Ombudsmen to further ensure that the Agencies and their adjunct Policy Juries conform to the public will.
- The Judiciary interprets the publicly enacted laws. Expert Courts arbitrate among individuals, organizations and the Expert Agencies.
- The public elects high-ranking executives. Candidate lists for public office are narrowed by public polls and the public makes the final selection in a general vote. The qualifications of the candidates are made public, but irrelevant aspects of personality, such as race, gender, age, physical appearance and personal charisma are not publicized. To achieved this the candidates run anonymously, through professional stand-in advocates.
- Issues of general importance or basic principle may arise not only from publicly submitted proposals, but also from the Expert Agencies and the Judiciary. Issues of major importance that arise from these sources are referred to the ultimate authority, which is the general public.

4.2 Defining the Referendum and Poll Issues

Defining the agenda (the list of issues selected for public vote) for referendums and polls is of central importance. The public itself must be able to decide which issues it wants to vote on, and which policy options it should be able to chose from among. Without this power, the public input would be limited to issues or choices that a ruling elite would allow. This would make public self-governance meaningless.

Public definition of the issues is achieved through the National Proposal Bank. Every citizen may propose (submit) three issues each year to the National Proposal Bank for consideration for vote in national referendums. The National Proposal Bank sorts and counts the proposals. The issues that receive the most requests will ultimately be part of national referendums. For example, the top five issues may be subject to public referendums, and the next ten issues may be subject to a Public Poll.

Along with each issue request, citizens can propose a preferred course of action. These proposals are also sorted and tallied by the National Proposal Bank. This activity is monitored by the Proposal Bank Jury, which is constituted and functions similarly to the Policy Juries.

In addition to requests made by the public, the Executive Council can also submit referendum and poll issues to the National Proposal Bank. In the model system, the Executive Council can request five referendum issues and ten poll issues each year.

The public also votes on a Budget Referendum that decides on the major divisions of the budget. Since there are many deserving causes and the main task of government is to divide the limited resources among these competing needs, the Budget Referendum is on a "pie chart" basis, proportioning the budget among major spending categories.

4.3   Public Debates and Information

Referendum Debates

Meaningful, rational self-governance can only exists if public decisions are based on true and balanced information.

To make well-informed decisions on referendum issues, the entire public must be educated on the issues being presented for voting. This is achieved through well-publicized series of Public Debates that precede the voting. Before the debates take place, the Debates Agency forms an Issue Panel for each referendum issue. The panels are comprised of experts who are advocates for each of the policy issue alternatives as well as independent members selected randomly from the public.

Issue Panels receive a list of the policy issue alternatives from the National Proposal Bank. These are the policy alternatives that were received from the public during the annual request for public proposals. The Issue Panel then extracts the most common alternatives from the diverse list of proposals and prepares the arguments *for and against* each of the policy alternatives. The Issue Panel also prepares the debate information for the public.

Referendum Juries supervise the actions of the Issue Panel. The Referendum Jury makes sure that the final policy options decided by the panel correctly represents the content of the public proposals. The Referendum Jury also ensures that the arguments for the public debate are factual and not manipulative.

Next, the material from the Issue Panels is used for the public debates that are organized by the Debates Agency. The conduct of the debates is supervised by the Referendum Jury and the Debates Ombudsman to ensure a fair, informative and non-manipulative presentation.

It is vital that the debate materials are made easily available to the public. Therefore the debates are made easy to access, and are presented in the mass media. The main issues and their arguments are listed in newspapers, information sheets and are also available on computer networks for easy reference and study in the home. To encourage viewing, debates may be combined with entertainment. Each issue is highlighted in the newspapers and on television on a specific "Issue Day." Indeed, the information is so prevalent that the average citizen does not have to make an effort to obtain it. On the contrary, it would be difficult for a citizen not to be informed.

Public Polls

Polls are similar to referendums except that polls are voted on by a representative group of the public that constitutes a statistically accurate cross-section of the general public. Polls are less expensive than referendums and the poll respondents can receive more detailed education about the issues than it is possible to communicate to the general public.

Preparations for Public Polls are similar to the preparations for referendums, but they are aimed at a much smaller voting audience.

The Debates Agency forms an Issue Panel for each poll issue. The panels are comprised of experts who are advocates for each of the policy issue alternatives as well as independent members selected randomly from the public. The tasks of the poll Issue Panels are similar to those performed by the Issue Panels in preparing for a referendum. They have to identify the issue alternatives and prepare the issue information packs. For those poll issue requests that arise from an Expert Agency instead of the public, it becomes the panel's responsibility to define the policy alternatives.

Voting in a poll is done by a group of Poll Respondents who are randomly selected from the public. The number of respondents must be large enough to represent the overall voting public. For example, there may be 2,000 respondents for each poll.

The Issue Panel prepares information packs for the poll respondents in the same way that debate material is prepared before referendums. The material is then reviewed by the Poll Jury and by the Poll Public Ombudsman to ensure that the material is balanced and not manipulative. Poll respondents are therefore informed before a poll in the same way that the public would be informed before a referendum. In this manner, a poll is a substitute for a referendum, but of course, at a much smaller expense.

4.4   Management by Expert Agencies and Policy Juries

The most important principle of Direct Democracy is that the government must comply with the will of the public. On major issues, the public will is defined directly by referendums and polls. Translating these general decisions into detailed policy action is done by the Expert Agencies. These agencies must always be conscious that they are not *making* policy, but *interpreting* and *executing* the public will. This runs against the tendency of individuals and bureaucracies who usually usurp power from the public.

A Policy Jury and Public Ombudsman are associated with each Expert Agency, which is designed to safeguard against this "power grabbing" mentality by monitoring the actions of the Expert Agencies. The role of the Policy Jury and the Public Ombudsman is to ensure that the actions of the Expert Agencies directly reflect the will of the people.

The size of each Policy Jury is large enough to statistically reflect the overall size of the population. For example, a Policy Jury may have 400 members who are chosen randomly from the public.

Policy Jurors receive specialized instruction in the Expert Agency's field of activities, e.g. health, employment, education etc. For this purpose, jurors serve as non-voting apprentices during their first year of service. During the apprenticeship year jurors receive balanced educational tutorials and materials from the Expert Agency. The jurors can also request and receive answers to specific questions about any issue within the jurisdiction of their Agency, especially about issues that the jury is debating at the time.

After their apprenticeship year, jurors serve for an additional three years as a voting juror. Each year one-third of the voting members are replaced by new jurors. This assures that the Policy Jury is always a body of knowledgeable people, which at the same time is also large enough to reflect a cross-section of opinions of the general public. In this manner Policy Juries combine true public representation with qualified expertise.

The jury works through teleconferences so that the jurors can work from home. The service involves one or two evenings a week. The jurors are compensated for their work.

4.5 The Public Ombudsman

The Public Ombudsmen and the Policy Juries monitor the actions of the Expert Agencies

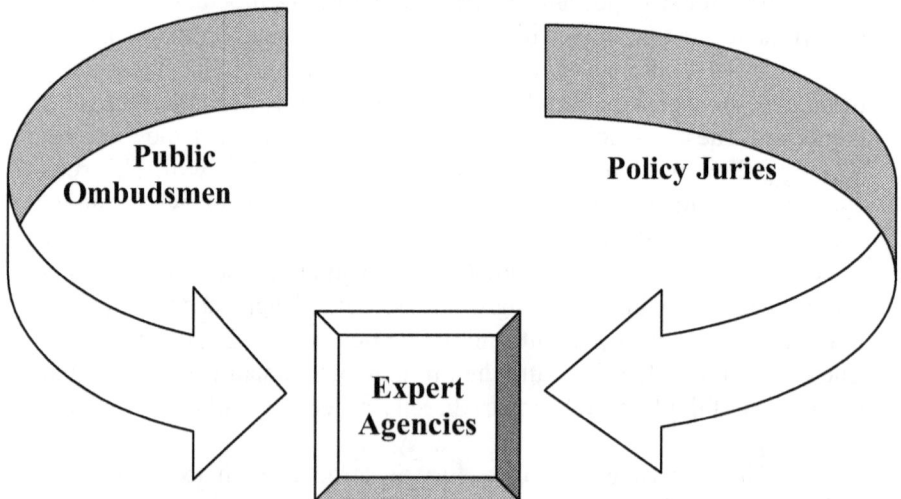

Public Ombudsmen

Policy Juries

Expert Agencies

In addition to Policy Juries, a Public Ombudsman is attached to each Expert Agency and Expert Court. The role of the Public Ombudsman is to ensure that Agencies and Courts act according to the public will. Ombudsmen also arbitrate disputes between the Expert Agencies and their associated Policy Juries. Public Ombudsmen can suggest corrective actions when they find that Expert Agencies or the Policy Juries are in conflict with the public will. However, Public Ombudsmen cannot formulate new policies and cannot enforce any decisions. If Public Ombudsmen cannot resolve their differences with the Expert Agency or the Policy Jury, they can refer such disputes to the Courts.

4.6   The Executive Council

There are occasions when emergencies arise that must be handled quickly before the process of public decision-making can take place, and, there are also major issues beyond the scope of any individual Expert Agency. Such matters are handled by the Executive Council, which is composed of the Heads of the Expert Agencies. The Executive Council also assigns the areas of policy jurisdictions to the various Expert Agencies and mediates among them.

The Executive Council must transfer the handling of emergency matters to the appropriate Expert Agency and Policy Jury as promptly as possible.

In cases of major public emergencies such as military attacks, revolutions and major natural disasters, the head of the appropriate Expert Agency will contact the Executive Ombudsman. The Executive Ombudsman will direct the necessary emergency measures and immediately call together the Executive Council to handle the emergency. The Executive Council can call an Emergency Referendum as soon as possible.

4.7   The Executive Ombudsman

The Executive Ombudsman handles urgent emergencies that require immediate responses until the Executive Council can convene. The Executive Ombudsman also chairs the proceedings of the Executive Council, but has no other powers. The public elects the Executive Ombudsman to a single five-year term. During emergencies, or as long as they have emergency powers, the Executive Ombudsman has the authority to command any emergency services, including the military, until the Executive Council can meet to take control.

The Executive Ombudsman *is not* the head of the State, indeed, the Head of the State is the public, and there is no individual with such a title.

4.8 The Judiciary

At present, a given court or judge may handle cases ranging from family affairs and criminal law to citizenship, banking, environmental issues, industrial patents, copyrights, computer fraud etc. Clearly, it is beyond any one individual to make knowledgeable judgements in all of these areas. This shortcoming becomes acute when each field is highly technical and requires specialized knowledge.

In the Direct Democracy model, the Judiciary consists of expert courts specializing in various areas of jurisdiction. There is a court that is expert in finance laws; another court is expert in technology, another in family law, etc.

The Judiciary interprets the law and arbitrates among citizens in disputes between individual citizens and an Expert Agency, and in disputes among the various Expert Agencies, Policy Juries, and Public Ombudsmen.

Decisions of the Expert Courts can be appealed to the Supreme Court. The Supreme Court is composed of emeritus Expert Justices and emeritus Chiefs of Expert Agencies and the Chief Justices of the Expert Courts. When needed, these members are constituted into Expert Panels to deal with issues that require specialized knowledge. Decisions of the Supreme Court can be appealed through proposals for referendums and polls to the ultimate authority, the voting public.

Decisions of the Supreme Court can be appealed to the ultimate authority of the voting public. Such appeals must be approved by the Executive Council, and presented to the public as one of the referendums or polls that the Executive Council requests each year. Evidently, only cases of general principle will reach this level of authority and public involvement.

4.9 The Election and Removal of Officials

The Executive Ombudsman, the Heads of the Expert Agencies and the Justices of the Supreme Court are elected by a public vote.

Candidates for each office must demonstrate at least ten years of relevant experience in their area of specialization. The Election

Agency selects eight preliminary candidates for each office, by lot, from the list of qualified and willing candidates. The public Election Panels may narrow the list of candidates or by polls that evaluate the candidates. The Election Panels are similar in composition and operation to the other public panels. Finally, the top two candidates for each office are presented for national vote.

In a fair system, candidates are chosen only by merit. However, human judgement may be affected by personal factors that are unrelated to the office such as race, gender, wealth, physical appearance and personal charisma. Judgements based on these factors are not fair for the candidates who are entitled to an objective appraisal of their opinions rather than the unrelated factors described above. It is also not fair for the public who may be mislead by such factors and may not choose the best candidate for the office. To secure fair elections, candidates run for office anonymously. Of course, the qualifications of the candidates and their views on matters relating to the office are presented to the public.

Officials are elected for a term of ten years. Officials can be removed by a 75% vote in recall referendum.

4.10 Symbols of Power

In a democracy power belongs to the public, and citizens must have an equal chance to experience the honors that symbolize that power.

For example, three citizens (and an alternate) are chosen by lot for a six-month term as Representatives of State and instructed in protocol. The Representatives of State sign international treaties that have been approved by the appropriate Expert Agency, receive foreign dignitaries, distribute awards, and in general represent the State at ceremonial occasions.

The trappings of power are a major inducement to power-seekers. This temptation is reduced when the trappings of power are dispersed to the public.

The symbols of power were also discussed in a preceding chapter.

4.11 Checks and Balances

The essential feature of Direct Democracy is that the government should comply with the will of the public. This requires that no individual or institution assumes too much power.

The bodies that manage public affairs are the Expert Agencies. The Policy Jury attached to each Expert Agency examines their main actions to ensure it complies with the public law. If there is no existing law derived from referendums or polls that covers a course of action, the Policy Jury should formulate the policy. The composition of the large Policy Juries represents the public and after Referendums and Polls, the Policy Juries are the next level of authority that can formulate public policy.

Referendums and Polls can cover only major issues, the main body of detailed public law will be derived from decisions of Policy Juries. In this sense, Policy Jury decisions play similar roles as court decisions in setting legal precedents, but they are even more authoritative as they are more representative of the public. In addition, the Policy Jury can also veto any actions of the Expert Agency it finds is not adhering to the public law and requires correction.

The Public Ombudsman provides a further measure of checks and balances. The Public Ombudsmen can also request corrective action if an Expert Agency, Policy Jury or Court acts inconsistently with the publicly set policy or law.

Disputes amongst citizens, Expert Agencies, Policy Juries and the Public Ombudsman are resolved by the Courts. Decisions of the Expert Courts can be appealed to the Supreme Court. Decisions of the Supreme Court can be appealed by National Referendums or Polls. Only major decisions that have general implications should be put to the public. To assure that this is the case, appeals to be decided by Referendums or Polls must be approved by the Executive Council which must make the appeals part of their annual list of five referendum and ten poll issues.

Even the majority vote in a referendum or poll may turn out to be patently unreasonable by circumstances that might arise after the vote. For example, if the policy received less than 60% of the vote, it can be overturned if 80% of the members of the Executive Council vote to overturn it. Such a veto can substitute another policy alternative or an existing law. However, such a decision must be subjected to a follow-up public referendum or poll, which can re-institute the original public decision by an 80% vote.

Other than this exceptional situation, a law passed by a National Referendum can only be changed by a National Referendum; and, a law passed by a National Poll can only be changed by a National Poll or a National Referendum. To assure stability, this can be done only four years or more after the original referendum or poll.

4.12   Amendments to the Constitution

The Constitution must be amenable to change, but only upon sustained demand by a large majority of the public. Amendment Referendums must be proposed by at least five percent of the voting public or proposed by eighty percent of the Executive Council. For an amendment change to the Constitution to appear on an Amendment Referendum it must first be approved by a majority of sixty percent in a National Poll.

Constitutional Amendments are only approved if passed by a seventy-percent majority in an Amendment Referendum. To ensure that the Constitution is not changed due to a temporary whim of the public, such decisions are subject to a second referendum held two years later. It becomes law only if confirmed again by sixty percent of the vote. Any Constitutional Law can be amended once within any ten-year period.

Evidently, these rules restrict the power of the public to make changes. Of course, these rules as well as the rest of the Constitution must be themselves approved by the public in the first place. It is likely that the public will accept restraints for the sake of stability.

Life evolves and society follows. Laws must be a solid framework for society, but not an obstacle to progress. The system must be flexible, though not fickle. Laws represent the codified will of past times and they must be changeable. The ultimate authority must be the public will as it prevails at any time.

Features of Direct Democracy

Referendums and Polls

Public Debates

Eliminates Linkages of Issues

Eliminates Linkages of Issues

Voter Forums

Part IV
Case Studies

D irect Democracy, as with other forms of government, will be tested by its success to manage human affairs. How does such a system in which everyone participates, makes decisions and resolves conflicts operate? The fictional case studies below illustrate how this system would work in real-life situations.

When Direct Democracy is implemented sometime in the future, three developments would have profoundly affected the human prospects. These are: biotechnology and genetic engineering, the move to space and weapons of mass destruction. Biotechnology in particular can fundamentally affect the world since it may change one constant against which all history so far has played out: human nature itself. This will raise many emotional issues.

Direct Democracy will be managed by every-day people. The reader may well identify with any of the following characters since anybody may find themselves in their positions.

Case Study 1. The Gene Therapy Act

This case study looks at the decision-making process using *public national referendums.*

Case Study 2. The 5th United States - Russian Arms Reduction Treaty

This case study looks at the decision-making process using *public polls.*

Case Study 3. The Budget Referendum

This case study looks at how the distribution of resources, i.e., major budget decisions, is *decided directly by the voting public.*

Introduction: The Referendum Schedule

<u>**Step 1**</u>   **The Referendum Proposals**

January - July

The public submits proposals to the National Proposal Bank.
Members of the public are entitled to submit proposals
(i.e., requests for a national referendum) on any subject to
the National Proposal Bank.

August

The National Proposal Bank collects all the proposals and sorts
them by subject, e.g., health issues, education issues,
defense issues, environment issues etc. Those proposals
receiving the greatest number of submissions are given
over to the Debates Agency.

<u>**Step 2**</u>   **The Debates**

August

The Debates Agency prepares the proposals for public debate by:
- Setting up Issue Panels for each referendum issue.
- Managing the public debates on the issues.

September

The Issue Panels Prepare the Debate material by:

- Receiving the proposals from the Debates Agency
- Wording the proposals so that they correctly reflect the
  wishes of the public
- Preparing information material about the issues
- Ensuring that that information reaches the public .

September

Referendum Juries review the wording of proposal issues by:

- Reviewing the work of the Issue Panels to ensure that the wording of proposals reflects the wishes of the public.
- Ensuring the debate material provided to the public is clear and nonbiased.

September

A Pre-Referendum Screening Poll is held if there are more than two policy options being considered for each referendum issue.

October and November

The Public Debates Period. Balanced and nonbiased information about each of the referendum choices is provided to the public. The information allows the public to make informed voting decisions.

Step 3   The National Referendum

December

The National Referendum vote is held during the month of December. The results of the referendum become law.

Table 3   The Referendum Process Timeline

Activity	Month											
	J	F	M	A	M	J	J	A	S	O	N	D
Step 1 Referendum Proposals												
Public Submits Proposals	▓	▓	▓	▓	▓	▓	▓					
National Proposal Bank sorts and tallies proposals								▓				
Step 2 The Debates												
Debates Agency Organizes Public Debates									▓			
Issue Panels Prepare Debate Material									▓			
Referendum Jury Reviews Wording of Issues									▓			
Pre-Referendum Screening Poll									▓			
Public Debates Period										▓	▓	
Step 3 The National Referendum												
The Referendum Vote												▓

Chapter 5
Decision-Making by Referendum

Case Study 1 - The Gene Therapy Act

Background

The major actors in this case study are Dr Julia Moreno, an Assistant Director in the Health Services Expert Agency; Philip Locke, the dedicated middle-aged Public Ombudsman attached to the Health Services Expert Agency and the one hundred and eighty members of the Health Services Policy Jury. Also participating are other officials and people from the general public whom we shall meet in due course.

To trace its history, genetic engineering started in the late 20th century. Despite the projections of the early scientists, the progress from carrots to sheep to humans was much faster than expected. Early in the following century the human genetic code was mapped and methods were developed to insert new genes into humans.

Once the means were available, the temptation fast emerged to improve people through eugenics. A synthetic gene that significantly increases muscle mass was developed for cattle and medical scientists soon developed a human analogue. Though reputable doctors would not introduce it, parents who had athletic aspirations for their children could find willing black-market practitioners.

The eugenic children quickly came to dominate the Olympics and other sports events. These young people profited financially from their genetic superiority and also became favorites of the opposite sex.

Success breeds envy and the situation soon came to a head. A group of "super-mutant" athletes, members of the invincible Las Vegas Machos football team, after beating the Baton Rouge Whites, were ambushed and lynched by a gang of Ameri-Klans, the self-appointed defenders of the old order.

5.1   The Referendum Process

Step 1   The Public Submits Proposals to the National Proposal Bank

The incident caused a great public uproar. We shall now join Jerry and Sarah Dermott in a conversation the likes of which was occurring in many households after the emotional television reports on the Ameri-Klan lynchings.

Sara: You know that I don't like violence, but I can understand their frustration. In a few years our children may as well forget about competing in sports if those "super-mutants" show up in every neighborhood. And, if scientists develop the "genius gene" our children can just forget about any decent professional job as well.

Jerry: Still, there are other ways to go about it. If those Ameri-Klans get away with this, you'll soon see liberals and ethnics hung up on every lamppost. We have the power to outlaw such violent groups and I plan to submit a referendum proposal to the National Proposal Bank to outlaw hate groups like the Ameri-Klans. With all of this publicity, I bet that we would have enough proposals to get this matter on the Referendum List for this year.

Sarah: Well, you can phone in a proposal, but I don't think the Ameri-Klan is the real problem. It's the scientists who don't know where to stop that's causing all of these problems. If we let them continue, regular human people like our kids and us will soon be obsolete. We can't let that happen.

Jerry: You can't stop progress.

Sarah: I don't call that progress. I call that genetic suicide and a disaster. There is already a referendum initiative to stop the irresponsible use of genetic knowledge and I'll add my name to the tally.

Jerry: Well, I don't think that you can stop technology, even if the referendum passes. If we don't do it, nature will, or the French or the Russians or the Koreans will do it.

Sarah: Let them worry about that. I care about our kids. I'll call in a proposal to stop this genetic improvement business.

Jerry: You wouldn't do that if our children needed gene therapy.

Sarah: This is not the way to cure people. More people will suffer if the mutants take over. I think I'll also submit a proposal to the National Proposal Bank.

We will leave the Dermotts at this point. We should inform the reader however, that like Jerry, thousands of citizens called the National Proposal Bank to request a referendum to outlaw hate groups such as the Ameri-Klans, and like Sarah, over one-hundred thousand voters requested a referendum to stop the genetic manipulation of humans.

After the wave of proposals to outlaw genetic engineering was received, people with opposite views started to submit opposing proposals. These were mostly from people who were disposed to genetic diseases and who were anxious that research should continue. These "opposing" proposals also requested a referendum on the issue, only they suggested the opposing alternative, i.e., to have the state encourage genetic research. Interested members of the public were able to follow the progress of both sides of the proposal issues on the Public Affairs television channel and on the internet. Numerous on-line chat rooms opened up to discuss the issues.

The Referendum Process
Step 1 - The Public Submits Proposals to the
National Proposal Bank

Public Submits Requests for Referendums

Public Submission of Requests for Referendums

- Members of the public are entitled to submit three referendum proposals per year.
- The proposals are submitted to the National Proposal Bank, which then sorts and tallies the proposals into similar categories.

By the end of July, all the proposals for the referendum list had been submitted to the National Proposal Bank and the work would now start to get the proposals and the public ready for the National Referendum that will take place in December. Proposals submitted after the July deadline would be considered in the following year's list of proposals.

Step 2   The National Proposal Bank Manages the Proposals

First during August, the National Proposal Bank sorts out the issues and ensure that they are worded in such a way that they would make sense to the voters and that they would be consistent with established legal systems. In September the Debates Agency prepares for the public debates which are conducted during October and November. And finally, the annual National Referendums and Polls are conducted during December.

The Referendum Process
Step 2 - The National Proposal Bank Manages the Proposals

The National Proposal Bank

The National Proposal Bank is responsible for:

- sorting and tallying the proposals that were submitted by the public and
- releasing the issues that will proceed to the referendum and polls, to the Debates Agency.

By the end of July the National Proposal Bank received over three hundred thousand referendum proposals about health and medicine. More than half of the proposals were related to gene therapy. There were also some other proposals about the funding of science programs, and the National Proposal Bank found that a few hundred of these would affect the practice of genetic medicine. These proposals were also tallied and grouped together along with the other proposals about genetic engineering. A proposal could be included in several categories if relevant. Altogether, over one hundred and eighty thousand proposals were related to gene therapy.

Once the proposals are grouped and counted by the National Proposal Bank, the Proposal Bank Jury examines the groupings and tallies. There arose a debate within the Proposal Bank Jury itself as to whether or not to include in the gene therapy tally, some proposals by religious extremists who, as in every year, requested to stop all medical services.

This year as always, the National Referendum held in December will include ten issues submitted by members of the public and five issues requested by the Expert Agencies. In addition, the public will also vote on the annual Budget Referendum.

5.2 The Debates

Step 3   The Debates Agency Organizes the Public Debates

The list of referendum and poll issues is now transferred to the Debates Agency, whose responsibility it is to prepare and conduct the public debates. As part of the debate preparation, the Debates Agency organizes a separate Issue Panel comprised of both experts (in the field related to the issue) and members of the general public for each referendum and poll issue. In some cases the proposals might have to be refined and reworded by the members of the Issue Panel, or they could even be supplemented with further policy options. If there were more than two policy options, the list of options would have to be narrowed down using a pre-referendum screening poll. Pre-referendum screening polls are conducted similarly to the polls described below.

The Referendum Process
Step 3 The Debates Agency Organizes the Public Debates

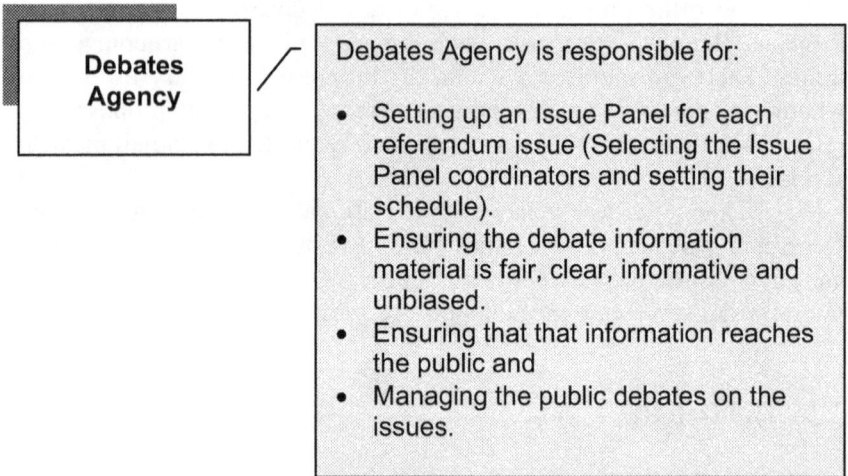

Debates Agency	Debates Agency is responsible for: • Setting up an Issue Panel for each referendum issue (Selecting the Issue Panel coordinators and setting their schedule). • Ensuring the debate information material is fair, clear, informative and unbiased. • Ensuring that that information reaches the public and • Managing the public debates on the issues.

Step 4   The Issue Panels Prepare the Debate Material

Issue Panels conduct the very important tasks of refining and rewording the proposal options and of preparing information packs about the proposals for the public. There is a separate Issue Panel to manage each of the referendum and policy issue subject areas (e.g. health, social issues, international policy etc.). This year the Health Issue Panel is coordinated by Elizabeth Smyth, who has already managed several poll debates. She will now coordinate her second Issue Panel for the gene therapy referendum.

Elizabeth's first task was to select the members of the Issue Panel. The Issue Panel must include an advocate for each of the main policy options that were extracted from the public proposals and two independent citizens.

In the case of the Gene Therapy Referendum the Debates Agency identified the following four policy options.

1.   To prohibit genetic interference with any life-forms;
2.   To suspend the research and practice of human gene therapy;

3. To allow gene therapy to prevent and cure diseases, but not for eugenic improvements;
4. To allow free research and practice of genetic engineering.

The first option came mainly from proposals inspired by the Genetic Heritage Society, a conservative group with a religious orientation. Upon Elizabeth's request, the society offered one of its Directors, the Reverend Adam Stolz, to be their advocate for Option 1.

The Referendum Process
Step 4 The Issue Panels Prepare the Debate Materials

Issue Panels

Issue Panels are responsible for:

- Formulating brief descriptions of each referendum option. These statements will then be used in public presentations, and also on the referendum ballots.
- Preparing the public debates information, this includes taped debates on the subject and detailed printed and video material that would be available to all voters.

Issue Panels are composed of 10 members

- Two representatives from the public and
- An advocate for each of the main policy options.

The task of advocating Option 2 was assigned to Steve Manning, a high-school teacher and public lecturer, who is also a well-known critic of gene therapy. As to the other two options, Elizabeth asked Professor Montes Serratto, a biologist, to be the advocate for Option 3, and Dr. Ida Noell, a pediatrician, to advocate Option 4. In addition, as the law requires, two representatives from the public were also chosen by random selection from the voting rolls, to participate in the Issue Panel. The two independent citizens selected for the Gene Therapy Issue Panel were Paul Gonzales, a retired department-store salesman, and Gemma Hirsch, a piano teacher.

The Work of the Gene Therapy Issue Panel

On the first day of September, Elizabeth Smyth welcomed the members of the Gene Therapy Issue Panel to Democracy Hall, the comfortable modern hotel and conference complex that is maintained by the Public Resources Agency, where the Issue Panel would spend the next two weeks. This might appear as somewhat of an imposition on the members of the panel, but Democracy Hall provides fine restaurants, swimming pools, sports courts and entertainment clubs. For most Issue Panel members, two weeks at the Democracy Center are a welcome diversion from everyday life.

Even before starting on their trip to Democracy Hall, members of the Issue Panel receive background papers on genetic engineering from the Debates Agency. On arrival at Democracy Hall, they spend their first two days attending presentations by experts in order to receive further education on the subject. These presentations also give the members of the panel an opportunity to ask the experts any questions they might have about genetic engineering, eugenics and related health issues. The Public Ombudsman for Health scrutinizes the material to ensure that it is presented in an objective and factual way, so as not to prejudice the members of the Panel.

On the third day, Elizabeth opens the panel session where advocates of the various issue options present their opinions and argue their views to the other panel members. In these arguments, members of the Issue Panel do not aim to convince each other, but rather, to use the discussions to clarify the options. At the end of the sessions, the panel formulates a brief statement on each option. These statements will then be used both in public presentations during the Debates Period and also on the referendum ballots. The panel also prepares a taped ten-minute debate on the subject, and detailed printed and video material that will be available to interested voters upon request.

One task that the panel did not accomplish however, was to narrow down the number of options to two, as is required for the referendum. It is preferred to have no more than two voting options for each referendum issue. Indeed, if more than two alternatives were voted upon in a National Referendum, a minority opinion could become the law, which is contrary to the spirit of democracy. Defining the two final options was accomplished by a pre-referendum screening poll

After considerable informed debate among the panel members, the final four remaining options and their justifying arguments, were revised and finalized as follows:

> Reverend Stolz Advocate for Option 1: "Genetic material is the very identity of a species. Although we understand now how genes work, this does not entitle us to interfere with our genetic heritage, whether it was the choice of the Creator to make us what we are, or ages of evolution. We are neither morally entitled to interfere with the product, nor wise enough to foresee the consequences. Genetic interference with any life-forms should be prohibited."

> Steve Manning Advocate for Option 2: "Genetic engineering may change human nature and interfere with it in unpredictable ways. Even if we can improve the next generation, we cannot foresee what such altered humans will do in turn. Human genetic manipulation should be prohibited. But genetic technology is vital for agriculture and industry, and it should be allowed."

> Professor Serrato Advocate for Option 3: "Ultimately, human genetic research may cure all disease. There are great moral and economic benefits in eliminating human suffering. We should not rush into applications, but we should find out what is possible. Therefore all genetic research should be allowed, but human applications should be limited to therapy. Genetic engineering to give people abilities beyond the normal human range should be prohibited."

> Dr. Noell Advocate for Option 4: "The history of evolution has imposed on us biological limitations, which we can now remove. Genetic research can end all disease, eliminate aging, and allow us to adapt to live in space where trillions of people can be accommodated. Also, genetic disorders are now common in the public, since medicine has allowed people with genetic disorders to reproduce. Genetic advances can turn us

back into a healthy species and then allow free progress. Genetic research, therapy and engineering should be practiced freely."

The four options were next reviewed by the Referendum Jury.

Step 5 Referendum Juries Review the Wording of the Referendum Options

Referendum Juries are attached to the Debates Agency, and contain one hundred and eighty members of the public. They are responsible for reviewing the wording of the issue options formulated by the Issue Panel and ensuring that the referendum options are consistent with the proposals that were originally submitted by members of the public. Both the Referendum Jury and the Public Ombudsman for Debates carefully review of all the options to confirm that they are indeed consistent with the spirit of the original proposals received from the public.

**The Referendum Process
Step 5 Referendum Juries Review the
Wording of the Referendum Options**

Referendum Juries	Referendum Juries are responsible for: • Confirming that the list of referendum options prepared by the Issue Panels are consistent with the proposals that were originally submitted by members of the public • Ensuring that the arguments for the public debate are factual and not manipulative. Referendum Juries are composed of approximately 200 members of the public.

Pre-Referendum Screening and the Poll Respondents

Since the Gene Therapy Issue Panel could not agree on which two of the four policy options should be presented during the December National Referendum, a pre-referendum screening poll was required to select the final two options. The pre-referendum screening poll was composed of 2,000 randomly selected members of the public; they are known as Poll Respondents. The poll respondents received detailed briefings on the gene therapy issue enabling them to make better-informed decisions on this subject than would the general public. A pool of 2,000 respondents is statistically large enough to reflect the overall view of the voting public. The material prepared by the Gene Therapy Issue Panel was used to educate the poll respondents about the issue options so they would be able to make informed choices. The poll was conducted in the same manner as all National Polls, about which more will be said in the next chapter.

In the end, the outcome of the poll eliminated the two extreme options, and the second and third options were selected as the two choices to be offered to the public in the National Referendum in December.

In Summary

By the end of September, at this stage of the referendum process we see that for each referendum issue the preparation work has been completed.

⟿ The Issue Panel defined the issue options.

⟿ The Issue Panel prepared packets of debate information material that is now ready to be distributed to the public. These information packets should ensure that the public is well informed about the different policy issues.

⟿ The wordings of the issue options were reviewed by the Referendum Jury and the Public Ombudsman for Health, and were found to be fair, non-manipulative and consistent with the proposals that were originally submitted by the members of the public.

⟿ A pre-referendum screening poll of 2,000 voting Poll Respondents, selected two policy options for the National Referendum vote on the Gene Therapy issue.

The scene has been set, and it is now time for the general public to get involved in the decision-making process. For the two-month period before the National Referendum, during October and November, the public will listen to debates and receive information about the referendum issues.

Step 6   Conducting The Debates

The most important point about the Debates is that they must be balanced, informative and non-manipulative. They must make the important arguments clear, in a simple way so that the public can understand them. And since people are passive, there must be incentives to attract them to pay attention to the debates and to become familiar with the debate materials.

A Fair Presentation of the Issues

Indeed, it requires some effort to avoid manipulation by advocates of the various causes. For example, emotional arguments must be avoided. In the Gene Therapy case the advocates of free therapy tried to paint the opponents as being opposed to all progress. The Public Ombudsman disallowed such arguments since they are derogatory, too generalized and are not strictly pertinent to the issue.

To prevent the unfair influence of special interest groups, in our model of Direct Democracy professional advocates who are trained in a factual, non-manipulative style, present the arguments for the various policy options to the public. People are easily manipulated by allowing influences of personality to be associated with the policy issue. In fact, in many cases in representative democracy the personalities of candidates, rather than their stand on the issues, often influence elections. Similarly, charismatic advocates could tip the vote in a referendum toward their side.

Public Participation in the Debates

To encourage public participation, it is imperative to make the information easily available to the public. Therefore, during the debate period, each referendum issue is highlighted for one week. The main arguments are summarized in three-minute presentations that are featured in all the radio and television news programs. Debate texts are printed in the daily papers, and can also be accessed by toll-free telephone numbers, with more detailed presentations available in public libraries and through the internet.

To encourage participation, attending the debates should be an enjoyable experience. One way this is achieved is by linking the debates with entertainment. For example, the debates are presented at the Democracy Center Theaters where free movies are played along with a ten-minute debate on the "issue of the week" played before the movie and during the intermission. Public restaurants are also popular places and people can enjoy discount meals while large screens alternate between debate tapes and short films.

With presentations in all the media, the debates are publicized so broadly that it would be hard for a citizen to avoid a basic exposure to each referendum issue.

But let us return to the Gene Therapy Control Act. The pre-referendum screening poll narrowed the choice to two alternatives. Both alternatives allowed research to continue, but controlled the applications of gene therapy. The two options are as follows:

1. All human genetic engineering applications should be suspended until the long-term effects on society are better understood. The main argument was that any genetic change, even for medicine, could alter people in unpredictable ways, which could lead to dangerous consequences.

2. Human gene therapy for diseases should be allowed, but genetic manipulation beyond the normal human range should be prohibited. The main argument was that curing people can only be beneficial; but, as in Option 1, changing people beyond their normal nature can lead to dangerous and unforeseeable consequences.

These arguments were publicized during the debates and the debate period, but could the public really understand the issues?

In 1990, the Public Agenda Foundation, a New York-based organization, studied the responses of experts, non-expert scientists and laymen to environmental issues. At first, the responses of the three groups were different; but once given a twenty-minute informative presentation, the laymen ended up with opinions similar to the scientifically trained groups. Evidently, a short informative presentation gave the laymen a grasp of the essential points. Given the basic information, the average citizen should be able to make informed and logical value judgements. A complete discussion of this issue can be found in the chapter "Can the Public Judge Complex Issues?"

The Public View on Participation

By and large, the public understands that voting in the referendum is a public duty, as well as an opportunity to exercise real power. This sense of power is an important human motivation and it will help to generate public participation.

Even so, people are passive. Voting must be made easy and pleasant, and must be actively solicited. To see the system from the public's point of view, we shall now join Sandy Morrison, an accountant; her husband John, a designer; and their twenty-year old son Matthew, on a drive to their weekend home in the mountains.

Matthew: Dad, could you switch to another channel? We already know enough about the Gene Referendum.

John: Actually, the debater on the radio just now has made a good point, if you would listen. Even if doctors only want to cure people, gene therapy could inadvertently lead to the creation of people with above-normal qualities. The effect would be the same as intentional eugenics.

Matthew: So what is wrong with that? That everybody will be healthy and smart and live for two hundred years?

Sandy: Although living to two hundred years sounds great, what will we do about children then? The world already has to accommodate more than ten billion people. Even if we start to build space colonies, we can't accommodate more people for centuries. Who needs two hundred year old people? And what if these new eugenic people will be too cruel and aggressive, and start a nuclear war?

Matthew: That is too alarmist, Mom. We are only talking about curing sick people. Any unintended effects can be stopped if things go wrong.

John: Maybe you don't know enough about it, Matt. Mom and I went to the free theater at the Democracy Center, and during the intermission the debater made some really scary points. For example, would you agree to compulsory sterilization if aging is "cured", and the world gets over-populated?

Matthew: Dad, I'm not ignorant, I checked out the genetic debates page on the internet and even took out a debate video from the library. I wouldn't mind at all living for two hundred years. In fact, if

Option 1 passes, I'll call in a proposal to change the law as soon as possible.

John: Well, at least we have a say in the matter. In the old days, the drug companies and the Medical Society would have flooded Congress with money to influence the passage of the laws that they wanted. Nobody would have asked us.

Matthew: By the way, Mom, I saw in the paper that your name was drawn to serve on the Food Subsidy Issue Panel. Will you serve?

Sandy: Well, of course, it's a duty, and one that I have actually been looking forward to. Since you can only serve on a panel once in a lifetime, why not? But it will also be nice to get away for two weeks at public expense. And if Dad joins me, we can get a suite at the Public Hotel, and spend the evenings together. The French Chef there is said to be the best in town.

Matthew: So far, I haven't been picked even as a poll respondent. I could use the few hundred dollars that you get for listening and arguing for a few evenings and weekends. And I'd be as serious about it as anyone. Do those computers that select the participants have something against young people?

John: You know that poll respondents are chosen by random. It's basic to the system that the respondents truly represent the public. But you will have enough opportunities to be picked, especially if you get your way and live to be two hundred!

At this point the travelers stopped for lunch and the conversation turned to other matters. We note that making an informed decision on a referendum issue, including the reading of a few newspaper debate articles, checking out the web pages and watching a debate video, occupied less than one hour in the life of the Morrisons. During that time they absorbed enough information about the main ethical and technical points to form informed opinions. Their decisions were free from pressure by special interest groups, such as companies who would have profited from gene therapy. They were not influenced by pressure or lobbying groups either.

Indeed, interest groups with huge financial backing can spend millions of dollars to influence a few hundred elected Representatives, but they cannot pressure or bribe millions of individual people. They cannot manipulate people through self-serving advertisements, especially since the Direct Democracy model system safeguards against unbalanced propaganda. This contrasts with representative democracy where special interest groups exert extreme pressure on Parliaments and

Congresses. The Morrisons, along with hundreds of millions of other people, whose lives will be deeply affected by genetic engineering, would have had little influence in a representative system. In Direct Democracy, they have the *final word.*_

The citizens of our Direct Democracy community have now had two-months of informative debate that has been free of manipulation by special interest groups and biased publicity. Presentation of the issues has not been influenced by charismatic personalities, where the essence of the issues is overshadowed by the personality of their proponents. It is now time to follow to the actual National Referendum vote.

5.3 National Referendums

Step 7 The National Referendum

After two months of well-publicized debate, the public is ready for the National Referendum. Voting is conducted during the whole month of December. During this time, the media refrains from any further publicity on the referendum issues, and privately funded advertising is also prohibited. In any event, the public has by now been saturated with the issues through as balanced a presentation on each issue as possible.

During the Referendum month, people can further consider and investigate the issues if they so desire. The media is not allowed to publish opinion polls on the Referendum and Poll issues until the voting has closed since these may influence votes yet to be cast. These are temporary concessions on the freedom of speech in the interest of unbiased public decision-making.

Voting is made as convenient as possible with several alternatives. People can vote at their local Democracy Center or vote from home through the telephone. The voiceprint library of the Election Agency is well equipped to prevent false votes. Additionally, people can vote through the internet using the secure identification system. Furthermore, on the last week of the referendum month, canvassers contact those people who have not as yet voted.

Of course, voters can vote on any or all issues, or abstain from voting altogether. Voting is not compulsory because it would be counter-productive to force arbitrary, indifferent and ignorant votes.

Returning to the genetic engineering issue at hand, we report here that in the referendum vote for the Gene Therapy Act, Option 2 won by 65 percent of the votes cast. After learning about the benefits and dangers of genetic manipulation, the majority of the public decided that ill people should be cured even if there was some risk of unforeseen consequences. However, proceeding to engineer "superhumans" would be fraught with too many unpredictable dangers. It therefore became public law that *"gene therapy shall be allowed, but genetic change of people beyond the natural limits shall be prohibited."*

5.4   Implementation of the Law and Conflict Resolution

Step 8   Expert Agencies are Accountable to the Public by Enforcing the Public Will

Laws encounter many unforeseen situations. Even in Direct Democracy, individuals must interpret the law and make decisions. The system must be so structured as to prevent bureaucrats and other individuals from accumulating power. The Expert Agencies must apply the laws in a manner that reflects the intentions of the voting public. In the Direct Democracy model the Policy Juries that are associated with each of the Expert Agencies, are responsible for major administrative decisions. Their members are representative of the overall public. Furthermore, everyday minor actions of the Expert Agencies are supervised by the Public Ombudsman.

Step 8   Expert Agencies are Accountable to the Public by Enforcing the Public Will

Expert Agencies	Expert Agencies are responsible for:
	• Carrying out the decisions and policies made by the public through referendum and polls.
	• Examples of Expert Agencies include the Health Services Expert Agency, the Defense Expert Agency, the Debates Agency and the Commerce Expert Agency.

Step 9   Policy Juries Monitor the Actions of the Expert Agencies

In our case study about gene therapy, the Health Services Policy Jury has 60 apprentice and 180 full members. Policy Jurors are elected randomly from voters lists. Each juror serves for one year as a non-voting apprentice, and then for three years as a full member. Sixty jurors are replaced each year. In this manner, the majority of the jury always has several years of experience in issues covered by the Expert Agency. Therefore, the jury is both representative of the general public and knowledgeable in the field of the Expert Agency with which it is associated.

Step 9   Policy Juries Monitor the Actions of the Expert Agencies

**Policy
Juries**

Policy Juries

- Are non-biased groups of citizens adjunct to each Expert Agency who are chosen at random and are statistically representative of the public at large.
- Are responsible for ensuring that the work of the Expert Agencies follows the public will and public policy.
- Give policy direction to the Expert Agency in cases where there are no existing laws about a subject. The decisions may direct the Agency how to act, or direct the Agency to request a Poll or Referendum.
- Monitor the actions of the Expert Agency and decide when the actions of the Agency conflict with the policies determined by the public.
- Have veto power over the Expert Agency with which they are associated.
- Resolve disputes between the Public Ombudsman and the Expert Agency.

Because the jurors would not necessarily reside in the same area, Policy Juries communicate through teleconferencing. Each juror spends about five hours each week on jury activities, usually during evenings and weekends, and is paid for this service.

Policy Juries monitor the actions of the Expert Agency and decide when their actions conflict with the policies that have been decided by the public. These conflicts may have been identified by the Health Services Public Ombudsman, the Health Services Court or by 20% or more of the Policy Jury members. The Agency itself may also ask for guidance from the Policy Jury.

The Health Services Policy Jury has veto power over the Health Services Expert Agency. The decisions of the Policy Juries *are law* and can be reversed only by a public referendum or poll. For such action, the case must be appealed to Executive Council, which decides whether to refer the problem to the voting public.

Returning again to the Gene Therapy Law, an unforeseen development soon materialized that required the action of the Health Services Policy Jury. Several years before the new law was passed by a National Referendum, scientists had synthesized artificial genes that suppressed multiple sclerosis, a previously untreatable, disabling and fatal disease. The nerve cells were the targets for the new genes, but in some cases the introduced genes migrated to other tissues, including the reproductive sperm and egg cells, and through them, into the patients' children. At first, scientists thought that this would only protect the patients' children from the disease, but when those children reached school age, it become clear that the artificial genes affected the children's nervous system in unexpected ways. The world started to take an intense interest in the matter when one of these gene therapy offspring, 18-year old Professor Talbert Shelton, won the Nobel Prize for Physics. This happened two years after the Gene Therapy Act was passed.

The question now placed before the Health Services Policy Jury was whether or not the use of the artificial genes that suppressed multiple sclerosis, but also effects offspring with seemingly beneficial side effects, contravenes the Gene Therapy Act.

Step 10   The Public Ombudsmen Ensure the Law is Followed

The Public Ombudsmen's Role and When Conflicts Arise Between Public Policy and the Expert Agency's Actions

Philip Locke was a firm believer in the right of the public to self-determination. After college, he started his career as a junior hospital administrator, and later spent a decade as District Manager of the Heart Association. When the position of the Health Services Public Ombudsman became vacant, Philip had the ideal background: an expertise in health management and no prior association with the Health Services Expert Agency. The responsibility of the Public Ombudsman associated with each Expert Agency is to ensure that the laws enacted through Direct Democracy are upheld.

Step 10   The Public Ombudsmen Ensure the Law is Followed

Public Ombudsman

Public Ombudsman

- There is one Public Ombudsman associated with each Expert Agency.

- The Public Ombudsman is responsible for ensuring that the laws enacted through public referendum and polls are upheld.

About five years before the Talbert Shelton story started to draw public interest, Philip's appointment was confirmed by the Health Services Policy Jury. Now, at the age of forty-four, Philip has seven years of experience as a Public Ombudsman adjunct to the Health Services Expert Agency behind him. So far, there were few disputes between him and the Agency that had to be referred to the Health Services Court and even fewer that had to be appealed to the Health Services Policy Jury. In fact, his record in settling disputes with the Expert Agency was outstanding, and on the average, only two cases were appealed each year to the Health Services Policy Jury. This was because the Expert Agency followed the public law scrupulously. Disputes with the Public Ombudsman arose from differences in judgement, not from corruption.

Even before the Gene Therapy Act, genetic diseases and cures had been a sensitive subject. This field grew more important as medicine allowed carriers of many defective genes to live normal lives and parent children. By expert estimates, over one quarter of the population carried genes for a host of diseases. At the Health Services Agency, the Genetic Medicine Division, headed by Dr. Julia Moreno, managed this important field of health services.

Dr. Moreno had met Philip Locke only in the course of a few routine policy audits by the Public Ombudsman. There was nothing in their pasts that could foresee the approaching clash.

Until the case of the young prodigy Professor Shelton, gene therapy for multiple sclerosis was a blessing free of controversy. It may have been considered even more so after its beneficial side effects were discovered; society could only benefit from an unexpected crop of geniuses amongst the patients' descendants.

It would seem that only a heartless monster could object to continuing gene therapy for multiple sclerosis sufferers. Philip Locke may have been a somewhat colorless administrator, but hardly a stonehearted monster. And yet, fate now meted out upon him the thankless task of interfering with medical help.

It was evident that gene therapy for multiple sclerosis had crossed the boundaries of the new law, although inadvertently. Over two-thirds of the children of patients implanted with the anti-multiple sclerosis gene had intelligence in the genius range. Statistically, this was clearly beyond the norm, and some of the "mutant" geniuses also reached levels of intelligence that experts found unprecedented. Inadvertently, medicine had crossed the line between therapy and eugenics.

The letter from the Public Ombudsman informing her that the use of gene therapy for curing multiple sclerosis must be stopped shocked Dr. Julia Moreno. During many years of medical practice, she had witnessed helplessly as multiple sclerosis patients withered and died. As a public administrator, it was most satisfying to make gene therapy available to all the afflicted patients. She also felt a parental pride toward the young geniuses who were the fortunate by-products of this advance.

The letter from the Public Ombudsman's office therefore appeared to Dr. Moreno as particularly evil. It was true that technically, the multiple sclerosis gene therapy conflicted with the law; but how could any sane person suggest stopping gene therapy and re-activating the old scourge of the disease? Only a myopic bureaucrat could believe that such was the intent of the voting public.

It wasn't with great pleasure either that Philip Locke had to reject Dr. Moreno's harsh reply. But to Philip Locke, the law was sacred. Evidently, the voters who passed the Gene Therapy law believed that society should forgo medical benefits to avoid the dangers of an unpredictable future. And in fact, the multiple sclerosis therapy presented just such a dilemma. A dreaded disease was cured, but who knows what dreaded weapons may be invented by the super-geniuses amongst those ex-patients' children? And what sorts of even more superior creatures may they engineer, and what will these do in turn, within a few generations? Indeed, human survival itself may be at stake.

In any event, the Health Services Expert Agency made a fundamental policy decision that acted against the will of the people. The Health Services Agency decreed that the treatment of multiple sclerosis sufferers using gene therapy would continue. The Health Services Public Ombudsman, who was appointed to guard against just this kind of action, was forced to step in to protect the decision of the people.

The Public Ombudsman could appeal to the Health Services Policy Jury or to the Health Services Court to stop the decision of the Health Services Expert Agency that allowed the continuation of gene therapy. The Public Ombudsman decided to go to the Expert Court first. Usually the Court is approached first, as action by a Policy Jury of 400 people is more demanding and expensive.

The Public Ombudsman Takes the Issue
to the Health Services Court

The Health Services Court was a typical Expert Court, different from the all-purpose courts of the olden days. In the olden days, courts and judges used to deal with miscellaneous cases that arose in their jurisdiction. This would present a judge with cases ranging from criminal and civil cases to highly technical subjects such as computer security and medical malpractice. Necessarily, judges had to rule on topics in which they may have been unqualified, lacking specialized knowledge or experience. In contrast, in our model system courts are expert in their fields. Judges on the Health Services Court for example, have medical or related education. Some were doctors or nurses, and all were given health services training, as well as legal training, before being allowed to sit on the bench.

It was the Health Services Expert Court that was now called upon to decide the dispute between Philip Locke and Dr. Julia Moreno. To be brief, the Court sided with the Health Services Expert Agency, and allowed the practice of using gene therapy against multiple sclerosis to continue, much to the distress of Philip Locke.

Philip Locke had not risen to his post for lack of tenacity. In his view, regardless of the merits of gene therapy, the larger principle of direct democracy had been violated. The next forum of appeal, the Policy Jury, was representative of the highest authority, the voting public. Significant issues such as this one require guidance from such a high public authority, and Philip Locke appealed the case to the Health Services Policy Jury.

The Public Ombudsman Appeals the Court's Decision to the Policy Jury

The Policy Jury agreed to hear the appeal because standard procedures require that when a jury believes a conflict exists between the law and an administrative policy decision made by an Expert Agency, a hearing should be convened.

In this case, the Chief Juror entered a Convening Note in the Jury's teleconference network to inform the jurors of the scheduled hearing. Along with this note, the jurors also received a brief by Philip Locke explaining his request for the hearing. Representing the other side of the issue, Dr. Moreno submitted her own brief advising the jury of her opinion that the public law explicitly permitted gene therapy, and therefore the jury's action was not needed. Indeed, she argued, the therapy saved lives, and this was in the basic the spirit of Direct Democracy, which valued above all human dignity and human life.

On the evening of the following Monday, the jury convened for a teleconference meeting. The majority of the jurors agreed that the case had profound implications and a jury decision was indeed called for. The jury voted to agree to hear the case.

During the next two weeks the Public Ombudsman for Health Services Expert Agency arranged a series of medical and legal experts to speak to the jury. This was followed by two weeks of deliberations among the jury members. Realistically, the actual discussion occupied only a few hours during these two weeks, as the jury usually convened only for two hours on Wednesday evenings and three hours on Saturday afternoons each week.

The arguments and deliberations of the Policy Jury were open to the public and interested people could follow the proceeding through the electronic media, at libraries and through computer network communication lines. We shall report here that the outcome affirmed the reservations of the public law about eugenics.

The Policy Jury ruled with the Public Ombudsman that gene therapy for multiple sclerosis should be suspended until a way is found to prevent the hereditary consequences.

Obviously, Dr. Moreno was disappointed. Yet the Policy Jury, an institution representative of the public, honored the letter of the law. But the case was so important, and the implications were so far-reaching, that Dr. Moreno decided on a further appeal that could lead back to the highest source of the law, *the public will.*

The Expert Agency Appeals the Policy Jury's Decision to the Executive Council

The Executive Council is the highest executive authority. However, even the Executive Council could not overrule the decisions of a Policy Jury which is representative of a cross-section of the people. But, because the action of a Policy Jury is not quite a public vote, it cannot be considered as the ultimate authority. For cases of general principle, there must a way to appeal to the voting public. This appeal must first go through the Executive Council. If the Executive Council upholds the decision of the Policy Jury, then the avenues of appeal are exhausted, except, of course, if the public itself reopens the matter through the submission of public proposals. If the Executive Council disagrees with the conclusions of the Policy Jury, it can refer the case to a referendum or poll. This request would then be amongst the five referendums or ten poll issues that the Executive Council requests each year.

Although appeals from the Expert Agencies through to the Executive Council are rare, Dr. Moreno decided to take such action. Upon consideration of the issue, the Executive Council found that in the present case, the law was self-contradictory: it allowed gene therapy, but ruled out eugenics, and had no provision where the two cannot not be separated. The precedent had to be clarified by the voting public. The Executive Council therefore requested a National Poll on the subject.

Returning to Philip Locke, it was his duty to uphold the public law, even when the issue he was required to support was against his own personal convictions. In fact, Philip Locke gained some public recognition through this case. While Philip worked to uphold the law, he could also act to change it. Indeed, while Direct Democracy entails public decision-making, it does not stifle individual leadership. To the surprise of many people Philip Locke started an action group to generate public momentum for changing the law. The publicity about his views helped to formulate the public attitude on the issue, and in this manner he may have had an important role in the outcome of the poll.

Direct Democracy is predicated on the belief that the majority of people have a respect for life and a sense of compassion. We are happy to conclude this case study by reporting that when the plight of the multiple sclerosis patients was subjected to a poll, the majority of the Poll Respondents voted to allow the cure to proceed, with the provision to intensify the research for cures that will have no hereditary consequences. And, since in Direct Democracy the public will as expressed by the National Poll becomes public law, the patients were promptly given the benefits of genetic medicine.

Conclusion

The Gene Therapy case study followed the course of an issue that arose from a matter of public concern and generated enough public proposals to become a referendum. We saw how the public debate was prepared by the Issue Panel, and scrutinized by the Referendum Jury and the Public Ombudsman in order to present balanced information to the public. We also saw that when a basic question arose in the course of the implementation of policy by an Expert Agency, the issue was first appealed through the Expert Court, then through the Policy Jury, and finally through the Executive Council which referred it back to the voting public in a poll.

Similar cases do of course flow through various channels in representative democracy as well. The difference is that in the Direct Democracy model, issues that are fundamental to the future of the entire public are not decided by politicians wheeling and dealing with pressure groups. Rather, from the inception of the law-making process, through to its implementation and interpretation, the people, the same public whose lives will be affected by the outcome, managed it. This is the best guarantee that the process will honor the dignity and the right for self-determination of every citizen, and that the decision will serve the best interests of the public.

Chapter 6
Decision-Making by National Polls

Case Study 2 - International Policy:
Arms Reduction Treaty

The present chapter will further illustrate how the institutions of the Direct Democracy model operate. We shall observe a poll that was initiated by an Expert Agency through the Executive Council at the request of the Public Ombudsman. We shall observe how the Poll Respondents are selected and educated, and how the Expert Agency then implements the decision.

National Polls are an important part of the Direct Democracy model. They are the second of three levels of public participation.

The *first level* of public participation and broadest in terms of the number of participants are the National Referendums. Referendums address matters of general principle by the voting public who is aware of the essential general arguments.

The *second level* is the Polls where thousands of Poll Respondents, who are a statistically accurate cross-section of the general public, vote on issues. The Poll Respondents receive more detailed education about the issue than it is possible to communicate to the general public.

The *third level* are the Policy Juries, which are composed of several hundred people and are also a representative sample of the public. Policy Jurors are well educated in their specialized area of government activity.

These three levels have decreasing degrees of general participation in terms of the number of people actively involved, but the participants have increasing knowledge of the issues.

Levels of Public Participation

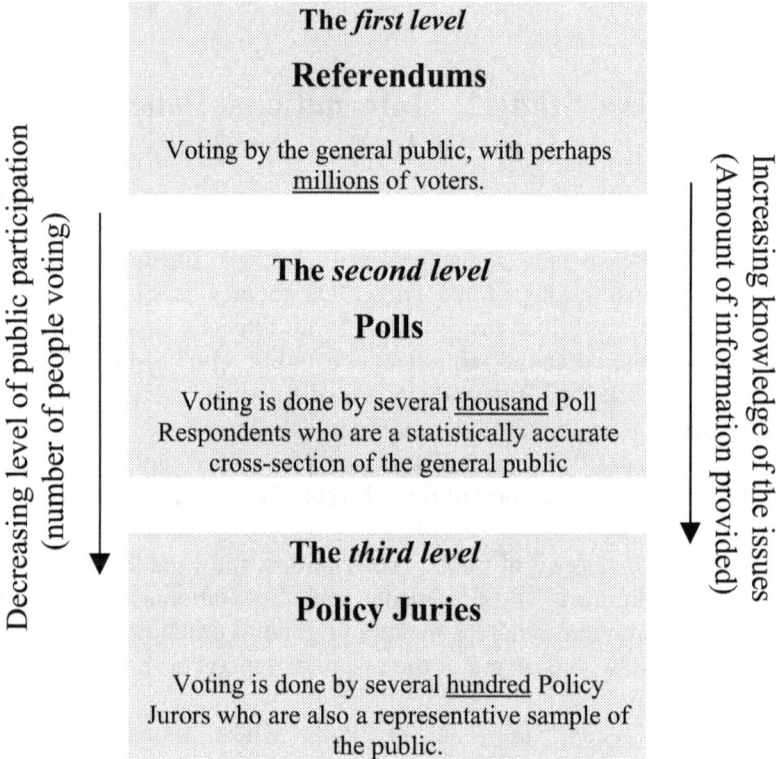

Decreasing level of public participation
(number of people voting)

Increasing knowledge of the issues
(Amount of information provided)

The *first level*

Referendums

Voting by the general public, with perhaps
<u>millions</u> of voters.

The *second level*

Polls

Voting is done by several <u>thousand</u> Poll
Respondents who are a statistically accurate
cross-section of the general public

The *third level*

Policy Juries

Voting is done by several <u>hundred</u> Policy
Jurors who are also a representative sample of
the public.

Background

This chapter describes a case that was decided through a
National Poll. As a background to this case, we should describe the
balance of nuclear weapons in the middle of the 21st century. The
preceding century saw the advent and accumulation of nuclear weapons
on a scale that could destroy humankind many times over. Following
the growth of these deadly arsenals, there also arose a powerful public
movement for disarmament.

The public attitude was reflected in referendums initiated in the
1980's by the Nuclear Freeze Movement. A freeze on nuclear weapons

to be followed by disarmament was favored by a large majority of voters in many states, counties and towns throughout the United States. However, these referendums and initiatives were not binding. The defense industry continued to make major contributions to political campaigns and in effect bribed Congress to continue the funding of missile programs. The arms build-up continued contrary to the public will. In effect, the corruption of the representative system allowed the growth of the senseless nuclear overkill.

However, toward the end of the century as the USSR dissolved into separate autonomous countries and Russia became free and democratic, the political differences between the superpowers decreased; nuclear weapons became unjustifiable. Environmental crises and nuclear accidents kept the issue in focus and economic problems made the weapons burdensome. By the middle of the 21st century, several disarmament treaties reduced nuclear weapons to one tenth of their past peak numbers.

At the same time, the smaller nuclear power countries retained and increased their arsenals. Not only did France, Great Britain and China possess nuclear weapons, but India, Pakistan, Israel, Argentina, Brazil, South Africa and North Korea each possessed hundreds of bombs; each of them became capable of devastating any other nation. But with a thousand warheads each and superior missile forces, the United States and Russia still remained the nuclear superpowers.

By now in our model case study, the Direct Democracy system of the United States and a democratic Russia had little reason to distrust each other. There was a mutual understanding that further arms reductions would increase the security of both countries since the chances of accidental war could be then further decreased. However, there was a basic problem with further disarmament. Further reduction would bring the arsenals of the major powers down to levels similar to the secondary nuclear powers. This decision could have major implications, and in Direct Democracy, that meant the need for decision by the voting public.

There was in fact a public law that required further progress in the plan to reduce nuclear weapons. This law was established by a referendum held several decades earlier, which called for the ultimate elimination of all nuclear weapons. The Disarmament Division of the Defense Expert Agency had to implement this law, and the agency had negotiated the first four disarmament treaties with the USSR. The Defense Policy Jury monitored these negotiations.

As the fourth treaty was due to expire, public debate ensued on the question of further arms reduction. On the disarmament side, dozens of peace groups were united under the Zero Option Organization. Zero Option advocated the total elimination of nuclear weapons and ultimately of all offensive weapons. The organization gained mass support after a crisis in the early 2020's that brought India and Pakistan to the brink of a nuclear conflict. The Zero Option Organization now advocated a fifth United States - Russian treaty that would decrease the arsenals of the two countries to a few hundred nuclear warheads. During the Proposal Period, January through July, thousands of Zero Option supporters submitted proposals to the National Proposal Bank to this effect.

On the other side of the issue stood the still vigorous military-industrial complex as well the America First Movement whose supporters submitted thousands of proposals to ask for a referendum to *strengthen the military* until the nation once again dominates the world.

The Poll Process

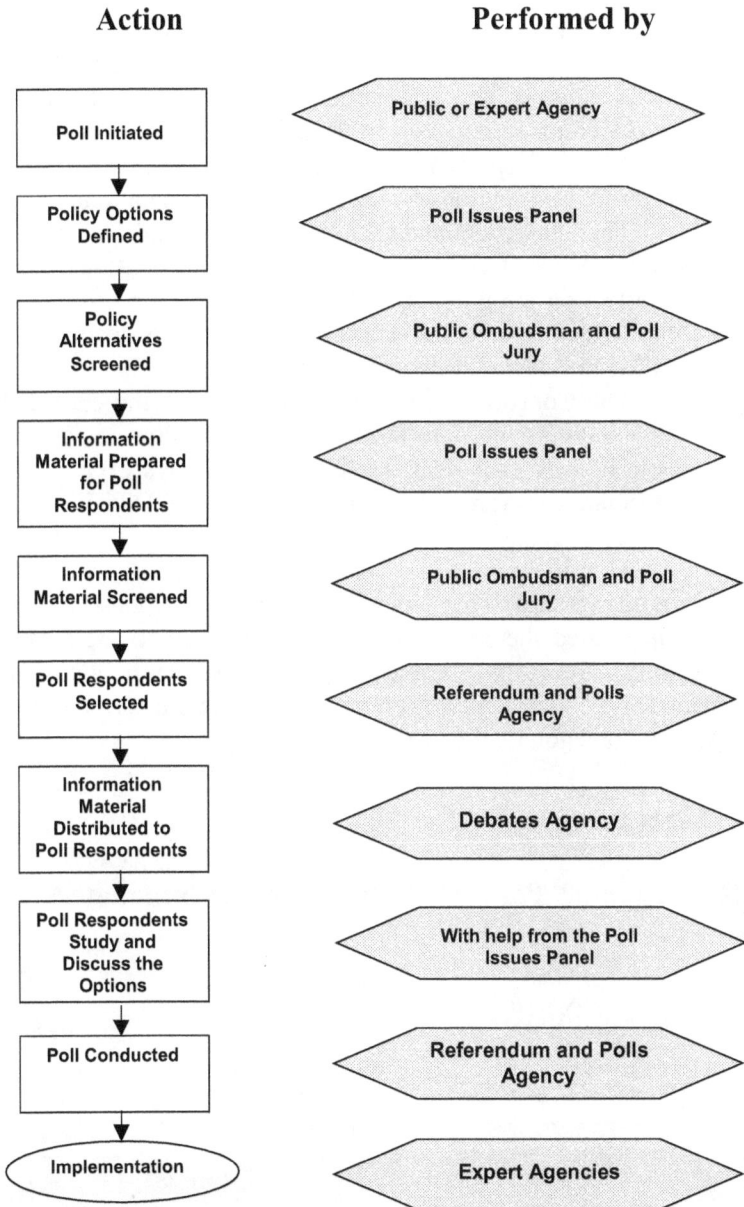

Action	Performed by
Poll Initiated	Public or Expert Agency
Policy Options Defined	Poll Issues Panel
Policy Alternatives Screened	Public Ombudsman and Poll Jury
Information Material Prepared for Poll Respondents	Poll Issues Panel
Information Material Screened	Public Ombudsman and Poll Jury
Poll Respondents Selected	Referendum and Polls Agency
Information Material Distributed to Poll Respondents	Debates Agency
Poll Respondents Study and Discuss the Options	With help from the Poll Issues Panel
Poll Conducted	Referendum and Polls Agency
Implementation	Expert Agencies

6.1   The Poll Process

Step 1   Requesting a National Poll

This was a year with many problems and millions of people requested referendums on a myriad of issues. The few thousand proposals relating to disarmament were too few to qualify for a National Referendum or Poll so under these circumstances, the Director of the Defense Expert Agency ordered the Disarmament Division to proceed with negotiations on the Fifth Disarmament treaty.

The Public Ombudsman for Defense had a different opinion however. The next round of disarmament negotiations could have a major effect on the international status of the nation. In the opinion of the Public Ombudsman the outcome of the treaty's decision was critical and called for the authority of the voting public.

The Constitution, which is presented at the end of this book, allows Expert Agencies to request five referendum issues and ten poll issues to be held each year through the Executive Council. The Public Ombudsman therefore asked the Disarmament Division to request a public referendum on disarmament.

The directors of the Defense Expert Agency were reluctant to honor this request. They pointed out that the Defense Expert Agency had negotiated the previous four treaties without public referendums and polls. The Agency argued that since too few public requests were made for a Disarmament Referendum, the public evidently trusted the Agency to negotiate the next treaty on its own.

What is the next step?

Referendum? Poll? or Defense Agency Negotiates?

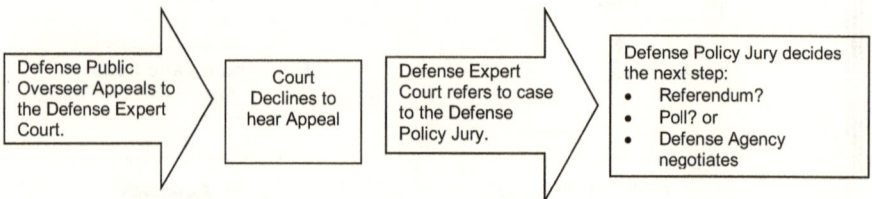

Defense Public Overseer Appeals to the Defense Expert Court. → Court Declines to hear Appeal → Defense Expert Court refers to case to the Defense Policy Jury. →

Defense Policy Jury decides the next step:
- Referendum?
- Poll? or
- Defense Agency negotiates

Referendum or Poll? The Defense Policy Jury Decides

The Defense Public Ombudsman was not satisfied with the decision of the Defense Expert Agency, and the first recourse available was an appeal to the Defense Expert Court. In the present case the Defense Public Ombudsman appealed, but the Court declined to rule on the case and referred it to the Defense Policy Jury. It now became the Defense Policy Jury's responsibility to decide if the issue of negotiating a fifth nuclear disarmament treaty should be the subject to a referendum, a poll, or neither. Note that in this case the disagreement was not over the issue itself, but whether or not to hold a referendum or poll about it. In cases where the disagreement is over a specific action, the Policy Jury can decide about the action itself or instruct the Expert Agency to request a referendum or poll on the issue.

At this stage, members of Defense Policy Jury were in homes scattered throughout the nation. They were notified through email to convene for a teleconference hearing. A week later, the jury convened at their home video terminals. At the session, the Defense Public Ombudsman presented arguments for a referendum on disarmament, while a senior official of the Defense Expert Agency argued against the need for a referendum.

The Defense Public Ombudsman's argument rested on the international significance of the issue. On the other side, the main argument of the Defense Expert Agency was that the Treaty would be highly technical and experts could negotiate more efficiently without public constraints.

The Defense Policy Jury debated the question in several teleconference sessions. As usual, many jurors requested and received further information from the Defense Public Ombudsman and the Defense Expert Agency. Jurors who had missed the teleconference sessions were given taped copies to provide them with the necessary information.

During the ensuing deliberations, the jury found the arguments of the Agency contrary to the Direct Democracy Constitution, which rests on the ability of the public to formulate policy. Nevertheless, the Defense Policy Jury offered a compromise solution: the matter could be subject to a National Poll rather than a referendum. In this manner, the randomly selected Poll Respondents would receive detailed briefings on the nuclear arms issue enabling them to make a better-informed decision on this technical subject than the general public. A pool of 2,000 Poll Respondents was felt to be statistically large enough to reflect the overall view of the voting public. This was indeed the very purpose of using polls in matters that required more detailed technical materials and understanding than could be disseminated to the general public at large. It was now up to the Defense Policy Jury to decide what the next step should be.

The Defense Policy Jury reviews the operations of the Defense Expert Agency

Policy Juries

Policy Juries

- Are non-biased groups of citizens adjunct to each Expert Agency who are chosen at random and are statistically representative of the public at large.
- Are responsible for ensuring that the work of the Expert Agencies follows the public will and public policy.
- Give policy direction to the Expert Agency in cases where there are no existing laws about a subject. The decisions may direct the Agency how to act, or direct the Agency to request a Poll or Referendum.
- Monitor the actions of the Expert Agency and decide when the actions of the Agency conflict with the policies determined by the public.
- Have veto power over the Expert Agency with which they are associated.
- Resolve disputes between the Public Overseer and the Expert Agency.

Even though the Defense Expert Agency opposed a poll on disarmament, it had to abide by the decision of the Defense Policy Jury. The Agency therefore asked the Executive Council to schedule a National Poll on disarmament.

This year, the Executive Council received requests from the various agencies totaling fourteen referendums and forty-five polls. Of these, the Executive Council had to select the five referendums and ten poll issues that would eventually be included on the public agenda.

The Disarmament Poll was one of the issues under consideration and it had several points that helped it move to the top of the issues list. First, the request for the Disarmament Poll had come to the Executive Council from the Defense Expert Agency by the decision of a Policy Jury. This has a higher priority than requests from the Expert Agencies themselves. Moreover, the Policy Jury requested it by a large majority. Secondly, there had been thousands of public proposals on the issue and although the number of public proposals was not enough generate a poll on its own, this, combined with the request by the Policy Jury added to the priority of the issue. For these reasons, the disarmament issue was indeed chosen by the Executive Council to be one of the issues included on the agenda for the National Polls.

6.2   National Poll Debates

The preparations for polls are similar to the preparations for referendums that were described in the preceding chapter.

Main Differences Between Polls and Referendum	
Polls	**Referendum**
1. Issue Panels formulate the issue options.	1. The policy alternatives come from public submissions to the National Proposal Bank.
2. 2,000 Poll Respondents who are randomly chosen from the public will do the voting.	2. The entire voting public takes part in the vote.
3. Because of the relatively small number of Poll Respondents, they are able to receive more detailed information on the issues than it is possible to give to the general public.	3. Information is informative but less technical.

The Issue Panel Defines the Policy Alternatives

As a first step, the Disarmament Poll is referred to the Debates Agency. Similar to referendum preparations, the Debates Agency assembles an Issue Panel. The tasks of the Issue Panel are similar to those performed by the Issue Panel in preparing for a referendum, but with an important difference: the issue arose from a request by an Expert Agency. If there are no publicly proposed policy alternatives, it becomes the panel's responsibility to define the policy alternatives. However in this case, there were many publicly submitted proposals from which the panel could formulate the policy alternatives.

To ensure a balance of opinions, the Disarmament Issue Panel has to include representatives of the various main points of view on disarmament. In this case, a director of the Zero Option Organization, a pacifist clergyman and a lawyer for the World Conscience Foundation represented the pro-disarmament side.   Speaking against further disarmament were a director of America First, a general of the Nuclear Defense Command and an attorney for a major weapons contractor. In addition, two citizens were randomly selected to join the Disarmament Issue Panel. They professed no strong views on either side of the issue and were the neutral public members of the Issue Panel.

As required by law, their employers released the members of the Issue Panel for three weeks of public duty. During this time they would stay at the Democracy Center in the Capital and work full-time on their project to define the policy alternatives (issue options) and to prepare the information packs and debate material for the Poll Respondents.

While the Poll Respondents were being selected, the Disarmament Issue Panel arrived at the wording of three policy options for further disarmament.

> Option A: "Nuclear forces should be reduced to 200 warheads on each side, deployed in a manner that assures the best stability."
>
> Option B "The fifth United States-Russian treaty shall equally reduce the United States and Russian nuclear arsenals, but keep them substantially superior to all other nuclear powers."
>
> Option C "No further nuclear arms limitations will be negotiated. The United States nuclear forces should be built up to superiority over all other nations."

The wording of the three issue alternatives were screened by the Debates Public Ombudsman and the Poll Jury, and were declared to be an unbiased and fair representation of the main reasonable policy options.

Next, the Disarmament Issue Panel, with the help of the Debates Agency, prepared information packages and debate material. The material consisted of a ten-page description on the state and capabilities of United States, Russian and other nuclear forces; the probable consequences of nuclear war given various levels of arms; the effects of arms reduction or build-up on the United States' status in the world, and on the economy.

The debate information material was prepared and before distribution, the Debates Public Ombudsman and the Polls Jury screened it. After requesting some revisions, these reviewers certified that the material was accurate, informative, balanced and non-manipulative. The material was then distributed to the Poll Respondents in print, on videotape and through the computer internet network one month before the poll.

Poll Respondents Study the Debate Material

Even as the Disarmament Issue Panel was preparing its material, computers of the Referendum and Poll Agency started to select the 2,000 Poll Respondents. The respondents were chosen from 300 million citizens, of whom about one-third were either below the voting age or excused for other reasons. There are 20 polls each year, each with 2,000 respondents with a total of about 40,000 respondents participating each year. In this manner, a citizen would have about one chance in a hundred of ever having this duty and cannot be a respondent more than twice in a lifetime. Even at that, participation was not compulsory. However, the duty was fairly easy, as Poll Respondents had to attend preparatory teleconference sessions for only a few evenings and for one weekend. The respondents were paid for this service. Therefore, few people refused to serve as Poll Respondents.

For the first two weeks after receiving their information packets, the Poll Respondents are responsible for studying the material and familiarizing themselves with the issues. During this time, respondents have to spend one day at their local Democracy Center to study the material that was prepared as video presentations. They can also teleconference with the members of the Disarmament Issue Panel and other experts whom they want to question. Poll Respondents are paid for this study day, and also enjoy the good meals and facilities that the Democracy Centers provide. Indeed, the study days at the Democracy Centers are considered a relaxing recreation, rather than an imposition.

While there were of course, no tests to check whether the respondents studied the material seriously, experience showed that the majority of people understood the importance of the issues, and fulfilled their duty with responsibility.

As in the referendum debates, professional actors present the video material during the poll debates. Actors are trained to present the material in an interesting but balanced and unemotional way to avoid biasing the issues by personal charisma and other factors that tend to influence people.

To ensure unbiased voting, the law also prohibited any advertising that may affect the Poll Respondents during the debate and polling periods. Moreover, by convention, the press also refrained from publicizing the issues during this time.

Returning now to the disarmament issue, the arguments for each option can be summarized briefly.

For Option A, the argument was that "200 warheads can still devastate any potential adversary and would therefore continue to serve as a deterrent to nuclear war. Indeed, a war on that scale could induce a nuclear winter that would devastate most nations. However, armaments on this level would decrease the number of people with access to the weapons, and therefore decrease the chances of accidental nuclear war."

Advocates of Option B claimed that, "After further limited arms reduction, the superpowers could still have up to a thousand warheads each. From this remaining position of strength the superpowers could deter smaller powers from starting nuclear conflicts, and also press convincingly for global disarmament."

Proponents of Option C claimed that "In a turbulent world, some nations could lapse into tyranny. Clear United States military superiority was needed to protect democracy everywhere."

6.3   The Poll Vote

Again, a situation arose where more than two policy options resulted from the Issue Panel discussions. Should these three options be put to a vote, there would be no guarantee that one option will emerge with a majority of votes. For referendums, pre-referendum screening polls are used to select the top two alternatives. However, since there are more polls than referendums, having a screening poll preceding each poll would be too costly. Therefore for polls, a Poll Preferential Voting System is used. Poll respondents vote by ranking each option as either their first, second or third choice. Respondents may also select to vote for only one or two of the options. In scoring, each first vote receives 3 points, each second vote receives 2 points and each third vote receives 1 point. The results of the respondents' poll of preferential votes reflected the nuclear worries of the public, and are as follows:

Option A was the   first choice of 1,085;
second choice of 514; and
third choice of 401 of the Respondents.

Option B was the   first choice of 498;
second choice of 1,173; and
third choice of 329 of the Respondents.

Option C was the   first choice of 417;
second choice of 315; and
third choice of 1,268 of the Respondents.

According to the scoring system, Option A received 4,684 points; Option B received 4,169 points; and Option C received 3,149 points. The public therefore enacted into law, through a Public Poll, that:

"The United States negotiators shall seek to reduce the United States and Russian nuclear arsenals to 200 warheads on each side, and these would be deployed in the most stable way, which was on submarine-based missiles."

6.4   Policy Implementation

Step 4   The Roles of Expert Agency: The Policy Jury, the Public Ombudsman and the Executive Council.

Public decision on an international issue in a referendum or poll is binding law within the nation, but it has no international force. The Defense Expert Agency, the government agency in charge of treaties, had to follow up by negotiating international treaties that would best implement the intent of the public vote.

In the present case the Disarmament Poll mandated the Defense Expert Agency to seek arms reduction to a certain level. Unfortunately, the representative system on the other side of the negotiating table was still influenced by its military establishment and insisted on maintaining its superpower status. Russia countered by offering a few options of their own: eliminating all space-based missiles but retaining a submarine-based force of 1,000 warheads; or reducing the submarine-based warheads to the desired 200 but maintaining 200 accurate and fast space-based missiles.

The Defense Expert Agency now had a dilemma. Since the publicly set objective could not be achieved, the Agency had to decide how best to approximate the public mandate.

The Defense Expert Agency judged that the Poll Respondents were aiming for stability to minimize the chance of accidental nuclear war. This stability would best be achieved by eliminating hair-trigger space weapons, even if this left more total missiles deployed.

Detailed decisions such as this one could not be submitted to repeated nationwide polls. However, this decision could be submitted to a Policy Jury, whose membership is broad enough to fairly represent public opinion. Therefore, before continuing with the treaty negotiations, the Defense Agency submitted its decision to Defense Policy Jury for approval.

The Defense Policy Jury Reviews Decisions of the Defense Expert Agency

There is one Policy Jury, comprised of 400 citizens, associated with each Expert Agency. Each juror spends four years on the jury, and one-quarter of the jury is replaced every year. In the first year of service the juror participates in the discussions but does not vote, and becomes a voting member in the second year. Therefore jurors on the Defense Policy Jury on the average, have several years of experience in dealing with defense matters, and are well versed in this field. Having been selected by random lot from the population, the group of 400 jurors was a large enough sample to represent the overall public.

After the teleconference debate, the jury decided to reverse the decision of the Defense Expert Agency. The majority felt that through the Defense Poll, the public expressed a desire for the maximum cutback of warheads, and the Defense Expert Agency should accept the second Russian option.

The Public Ombudsman for Defense Reviews the Decisions

A Policy Jury of 400 citizens is representative of the general public and is therefore a higher authority than the Expert Agencies or the Expert Courts. Nevertheless, the dispute between the Defense Expert Agency and the Defense Policy Jury indicated that there was doubt about the intent of the voting public. Before the matter could be considered finally resolved, the matter had to be reviewed by the Public Ombudsman for Defense. In this case, the Public Ombudsman interpreted the intent of the publicly enacted law in same manner as the Defense Expert Agency rather than the Defense Policy Jury. With this decision, the Defense Expert Agency could now turn the matter that originated from the Executive Council, to the ultimate authority, the voting public.

The Executive Council's Instructions

This year the Executive Council had more than twenty poll requests brought to it by the various Agencies and Ombudsmen. Most of these were new issues that had not been subject to a recent public vote. In this situation, the Executive Council felt that the two negotiating points proposed by the Russians fairly well approximated the public's desire for further stability and disarmament. Therefore the Executive Council declined the request for a new public poll on the issue. In this situation, the binding decision of the Defense Policy Jury, the last semi-public body, was the policy that the Defense Expert Agency was required to follow. The Defense Expert Agency was therefore instructed to accept the second Russian offer for the next round of treaty negotiations.

In addition to the missile cutback, the Fifth Treaty included missile verification procedures, limits on new weapons technology and other related matters. Before signing this major treaty, the final version was once again approved by the Defense Policy Jury and the Public Ombudsman for Defense, and finally by the Executive Council. All of these authorities verified that the new treaty would be consistent with the wishes of the voting public as expressed in related referendums and polls in the past.

The last ceremonial step in the process was the official signing of the Treaty by the representatives of the two nations. At the signing ceremony, the Russian government was represented by their President and Minister of Defense. The self-governing citizenry of the Direct Democracy of America was represented by a television repairman from Tennessee and a school teacher from Idaho, who were selected randomly from the voters list, to sign the treaty.

The further history of nuclear disarmament is beyond the scope of this book. For our purposes, the above episode illustrates how a complex foreign relations issue could be handled through the institutions of Direct Democracy.

Chapter 7
The Budget Referendum

Case Study 3
The Budget Referendum of the Year 2028

The distribution of resources through government budgets by its very nature influences the direction society progresses. Since budget decisions often involve ethical and cultural considerations, in true democracy this should be decided directly by the voting public, at least as to the major divisions of the budget.

All decent governments want the best for their people, but the main dilemma is how to best divide limited resources. Governments are often criticized for not adequately supporting worthy causes such as health, education, the elderly, public safety, the environment, the arts etc. Yet the same critical public would not ordinarily agree to pay more taxes for these purposes. If people wish to have true democracy, each voter will have to face these basic dilemmas.

In the Direct Democracy model, the public can control the budget in several ways. First, the Constitution requires that major divisions of the national budget should be decided by Budget Referendums. Secondly, through the usual proposal system, the public can request referendums on special projects that require large financial output. In referendums involving projects where large sums of government funding are required, the public has to decide the source of funding for these projects such as a special tax, or specified cuts in other spending. Budget proposals, as other proposals, can also originate from the Expert Agencies through the Executive Council.

Beyond the division of the budget into the main categories, Administrations must annually budget for millions of individual items. These budgeting decisions are part of the Expert Agency's responsibilities and are controlled by the public through the Policy Juries and the Public Ombudsman as described above.

Public decision on the budget is achieved through the two-part annual Budget Referendum. The first part asks the public to vote on the major divisions of government expenditure on a percentage basis in a "pie chart" form. The second part asks whether the total tax level should remain unchanged or if a change is requested, in what direction that change should take and the percent of change.

The Budget Referendum uses computers to record votes. As voters make a change in one item, the computer re-balances the rest of the items to add up to 100%. In this way voters can see how each change affects the overall budget, and can continue to make changes until they feel they have achieved their desired distribution. Ultimately, the result is calculated by averaging the budgets of all the voters. In filling out Part 1, voters use the last budget as a starting point to decide the percentages for the next budget.

An example of a Budget Referendum may be as follows.

Budget Referendum

Part 1. Below is the division of the budget for the last three years. Voters indicate the desired division for the next three years.

Budget Category	Previous Budget	Next Budget
Social Security and other Retirement	34%	
Defense and Foreign Affairs	16%	
Interest on the National Debt	14%	
Human Development	18%	
Family aid	5%	
Environmental protection	3%	
Government and Law Enforcement	6%	
Scientific Research	2%	
Other Programs	2%	
Total	100%	

Budget Referendum

Part 2. Below is the tax structure for last year. Voters indicate the tax structure for next year

Budget Category	Previous Budget	Next Budget
Annual Income		
Individual income below $25,000	15%	
Individual income above $25,000	25%	
Corporate income	20%	
Property tax / $10,000 of value	$100.	

As public interests change, voters may cause large funding shifts. This would be disruptive since the government must be able to plan for the future, honor existing commitments and support employees on a continuing basis. To this effect, Budget Referendums are held only every third year. The shift to the new budget is implemented by a gradual shift over the next three years. In this manner the Expert Agencies can plan ahead for a smooth evolution of their budgets. Furthermore, the public can pass laws to impose limits on the rate of change. For example, the funding of each main category may be allowed to change by at most 5% of its previous value (e.g., Human development may change from 18% to 19% or 17% at most but not to 3%). If the Budget Referendum results in larger changes, the results are adjusted to stay within the allowed rate of change. Keeping the vote from exceeding the 5% maximum shift is done at the level of the individual voter; the computer will not accept larger changes than allowed when the voter fills out the Budget Referendum.

It may be feared that the public will not want to tax itself at all. However, most opinion polls show that people understand the need for government services and are willing to pay reasonable rates. Even where Public Initiatives exist, such as in California, tax revolts did not eliminate state taxes. On the other hand, the public wants efficient use of its funds. Under Direct Democracy, the Expert Agencies are accountable to the public and there are no secrets. The public knows exactly what it gets for its tax dollars. The fact that everyone shares in making decisions on taxation levels will make people more willing to actually pay them. As with all public decisions, the decision on taxation belongs to the people.

Part V
Transition to Direct Democracy

Chapter 8
Hybrid Systems

The preceding chapters described a model system designed for maximum public involvement. However, the public itself may want an "intermediate" system with more representative and fewer direct features. Such hybrid systems would be needed during the transition period from representative to Direct Democracy. Indeed, most existing systems have both direct and representative elements in them, not unlike the model system described in this book. Various combinations may be suitable for different societies and for governments on local, national or international levels.

Social transitions are naturally slow and must develop against the inertia of existing systems. Therefore, it is important to realize that Direct Democracy measures can easily be incorporated into existing systems without disrupting government or social institutions. Improvement can initially be achieved by introducing the increased use of referendums and initiatives. It could also be mandated, even in representative systems, that certain major issues such as constitutional changes, major divisions of the budget, major foreign treaties and major ethical issues must be subject to referendums. A similar situation already exists in Switzerland.

An additional feature of Direct Democracy that can be incorporated into existing system is the use of Voters Panels that would be adjunct to the existing Government Departments or Ministries. Citizen panels would operate in a similar manner to the Policy Juries in the model system. The members of the panels are drawn randomly from the population and comprise enough members, at least one hundred, to be statistically representative of a cross-section of the public. As with the Policy Juries, the panel members receive general tutoring in the area of the panel's expertise. They would vote on general policy guidelines for their Ministry and screen major ministerial decisions, with veto powers. In this manner the panels can add public input and scrutiny to the existing system. Ultimately, these panels can evolve to have the same powers as the model system's Policy Juries.

However, the increased used of initiatives, referendums and Voters Panels adjunct to Government Departments would require substantial changes in the existing system. Because the very politicians whose power would be diminished must make these changes, this may cause major problems. For example, national public initiatives have never been seriously considered in Great Britain, the United States and many other representative democracies.

It may appear that conversion to Direct Democracy requires fundamental changes to the structure of representative systems. Surprisingly however, these fundamental changes can be achieved readily and without any changes at all to the existing systems. It can be achieved simply by electing Direct Democracy Representatives. This will be described in the following chapter.

Chapter 9
Direct Democracy Parties and Representatives

True Direct Democracy can be accomplished within the framework of a representative system and without any changes whatsoever to its structures and institutions. How can this be accomplished? By simply electing Direct Democracy representatives and parties who act in office according to this simple principle:

> *"I shall vote in Congress (or Parliament) on every major issue according to the majority decision of my constituents."*

In this manner, the public can assume true power simply by electing Direct Democracy candidates. Once elected, *every* Direct Democracy Representative will act on *every* major issue according to the *majority decision* of the electorate. As the number of these elected representatives becomes the majority in the legislature, and/or when they advance to positions of Prime Minister or President, government policy will automatically start to conform to the public will. Eventually this form of Direct Democracy can be implemented without any changes to existing representative structures. Direct Democracy Representatives can be elected and function in Parliaments or Congress, as other representatives.

This approach also gives the public an easy choice between the two systems by using the ballot box. If voters are satisfied, they will continue to elect Direct Democracy Representatives. Of course, if they want to return to the conventional system, they can simply elect representatives from other political parties.

The concept of representatives vowing to vote according to the majority views of their constituents may seem new, especially when we are used to the situation where representatives often act as they please. Yet this was not always the case. In earlier times in both England and The United States, people did recognize their natural rights to participate in decision making in a democracy. Some members of the English Parliament came close to making the Direct Representative pledge, and the right of people to instruct their representatives was embodied in several American State Constitutions. Technology now allows the people to reassert these lost rights.

How will Direct Democracy Representatives Act?

1. Defining the Issues

In the first place, campaigning as Direct Democracy Representatives will be the most efficient way to publicize the principles of Direct Democracy. We found a great response to our model campaign in Maryland. Even if it will require several tries for Direct Democracy Representative Candidates to win a seat in Congress or Parliament, much is accomplished by informing the public about this approach to true democracy. The campaigns can also highlight the public will on current issues and define the issues that most concern the electorate.

When elected, each representative will mail a questionnaire to their constituents calling for issues on which electorate-wide referendums or polls should be held.

At the same time a Voters Panel of approximately 200 citizens, or as many as needed for a fair statistical sample of the electorate, will be chosen by random selection. The Voters Panel will provide ongoing input that represents the views of the overall constituency, throughout the representative's tenure. Membership in the Voters Panel will be rotated, with half its number being exchanged every six months for another randomly chosen panel of citizens. In this manner, many citizens will have the opportunity to provide direct input into the selection of referendum and poll issues. Voters Panels may function through meetings in person or through teleconferencing. Its members may form specialized committees concerned with specific issue areas e.g., health, education, foreign affairs, etc.

Voters Panels will extract from public surveys, those major issues on which district-wide referendums or polls should be held. In addition, representatives will always submit to electorate-wide referendums or polls issues of obvious major significance, such as:

- constitutional amendments;
- life-and-death issues, such as abortion, euthanasia, death penalty;
- war-and-peace issues such as military draft; declaration of war; peace treaties; major weapons systems; arms control

treaties; major items in the defense budget;

- environment and conservation issues: major purchases, sale and use of government lands; clean air and water acts; clean-up of toxic waste; development of new energy sources; radioactive waste disposal;
- major agricultural subsidies; import quotas and tariffs; major public works.

Also legislation on national crises and issues that receive major media coverage will automatically be subject to polls.

How the public lets their Direct Democracy Representatives know how to vote for them

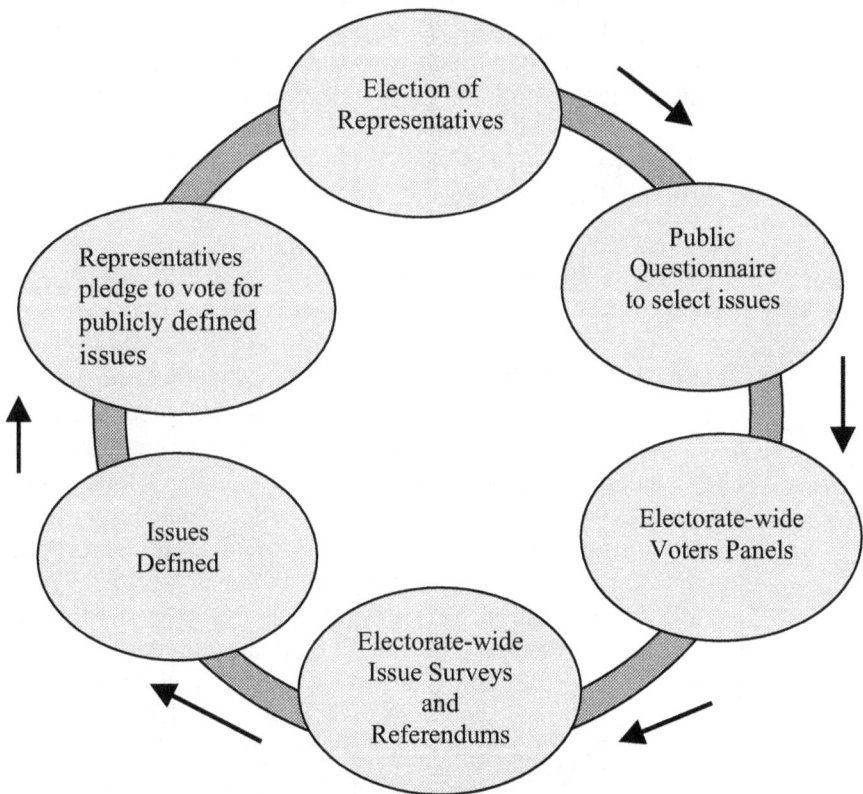

2. Public Referendums and Polls

Step 1   Define the Issues

> Once the major issues are defined, Representatives in cooperation with Voters Panels, prepare questions for the public to consider including alternative issue options for the referendums and polls. It is important that these alternative options are worded in a fair way. The wording of each alternative option must be approved as balanced and unbiased by 70% of the Voters Panel.

Step 2   Conduct Electorate-Wide Referendum and Polls

> Representatives will conduct electorate-wide referendums and opinion polls to identify those policy options the majority of their constituents choose to support. If there are no means to conduct referendums, all the major issues may be subject to public polls instead. On lesser issues that are raised by smaller numbers of the public or the Voters Panel, the Panel itself will debate and define the policy.

Step 3   Representatives Use Referendum and Polls to Select Issues

> Referendums, polls and the Voters Panels should be organized as soon as possible after the Representative is elected, to select those issues that will become the Representative's platform in Parliament or Congress. It is important to note that although the Representative may not agree entirely with the outcomes of the referendums and polls, being elected to decide issues according to the "*majority view of my electorate*" they will be ethically (if not legally) obliged to do so. As new issues arise during the term of the representative, they will be treated similarly. Voters Panels, the media and the public itself, will thoroughly scrutinize the voting record of their Representatives to ensure that they follow these guidelines as closely as possible.

Step 4   Continuous Communication and Feedback of Issues

Representatives will be accessible to the public through direct contact, public meetings and by regular communication and reports sent to the electorate. Through these contacts, the Representative will continually educate the electorate on the issues that arise in Parliament or Congress, while always being kept aware of public attitudes. In these on-going and direct contacts with the public, Representatives will present balanced information on the issues, although Representatives are certainly entitled to express their own ideas and preferences. Representatives will continually report their actions in Parliament or Congress to the public and explain how they have conformed to the public input. The public and Voters Panels will be able to continually scrutinize their Representatives to ensure that they are following the constituents' guidelines as closely as possible.

In short, the main job of Representatives will be to constitute a channel in both directions between the Parliament and the electorate.

3. Public Initiatives

Representatives will continue to make it possible for the public to continue to raise issues of its concerns after the initial referendums and polls are concluded. Following a request signed by 5% of the electorate, the Representative will conduct a poll and act upon the results in Parliament. This will enable members of the public to initiate new legislation.

4. Public Debates

Direct Democracy systems should provide the people with the resources to make informed and well-reasoned decisions. Before electorate-wide referendums take place, information is disseminated to all the voters in the district. The information must be balanced and unbiased. The policy choices offered must accommodate all the reasonable alternatives.

Poll Respondents are similarly informed. The respondents for a given poll are drawn from the general public voting lists and are provided with relevant information about the poll issues and alternatives. The voting information packs are prepared jointly by advocates of all of the policy options, and scrutinized for balance by the Voters Panel. The information will be mailed to the poll respondents well in advance of the poll, to allow for a reasonable study period. Study material will also be available through computer communication links.

5. Eliminating Special Interests

Public decision-making through Direct Democracy Representatives will prevent the influence of pressure groups. It will be impractical for pressure groups, political action committees and privately supported lobbying groups, to bribe the general public for its votes either directly or by huge campaign contributions in the way they currently influence politicians. Back room vote trading will be impossible where the representative's vote has already been bound by public decisions.

To prevent pressure on poll respondents, voting by the respondents will be anonymous, though carefully scrutinized by qualified independent auditors. Similarly, to avoid pressure on members of the Voters Panel, voting in the Panel will be anonymous.

6. Direct Democracy Parties in Proportional Representation Systems

Although this chapter describes how representatives elected under regional representation actively seek the consensus of their constituents in the formulation of their platform of policies and their voting patterns, the same applies to proportional representation. In a proportional representative system, a Direct Democracy Party could run for election and send its delegation to Parliament. The surveys, referendums and polls that the Direct Democracy Party would conduct to define the public's agenda, would be conducted nationwide.

The members of the Voters Panel would be chosen randomly from the electorate nationwide and would probably conduct its business by teleconferencing. It may be possible to choose several Voters Panel chapters that can convene locally in certain areas and then electronically tally the votes of all of the chapters.

Of course, a Direct Democracy Party is not a political party in the usual sense in that it lacks an issue platform of its own. It is purely a vehicle to carry the decisions of the public into Parliament until a more direct form of Direct Democracy, as described in the model system in this book, can be established.

7. The Mechanism for Conducting Referendum and Polls

Conducting referendums and polls requires significant resources. In the United States, Representatives would need to dedicate much of their staff to these activities. In regional representative systems where Representatives have small staff, there will be a greater reliance on volunteers. If several Direct Democracy Representatives are elected from various districts, they could pool their resources and conduct one joint referendum or poll throughout their districts (if the voters approve of this system).

In proportional representation, these activities are easier because there is only one Direct Democracy Party with nationwide membership and resources, and only one referendum or poll is needed on each issue, rather than polling each district separately.

When many Direct Democracy Representatives are elected, they will be able to pass legislation that will provide enough resources to conduct all the public surveys, referendums and polls as needed.

8. Nomination and Integrity of Direct Democracy Candidates

Just as every citizen has the right to be fairly represented in Congress or Parliament, so too should everyone have a fair chance to represent the public. It is of course important that the Direct Democracy Representatives who enter Congress or Parliament are competent to serve in government. However, they do not need to be professional politicians who may be driven by power. Direct Democracy Representatives only have to make sure to obtain and interpret the public view as formulated through polls and Citizens Panels. Qualified members of the public can successfully fulfil this role.

For each citizen to have a fair chance to represent the public, representatives should be chosen by lot from a broad list, possibly from a list of all voters. Selection by lot is also desirable for an additional reason. Especially in the early days of Direct Democracy opportunists or zealots may seek leading positions as Direct Democracy Representatives. Once elected such people may use their position to promote their own causes or to build personal political power. Such opportunists would discredit the Direct Democracy movement. These problems were pointed out through personal experience by Keith Mortensen, a Direct Democracy advocate in Australia.

If Direct Democracy Representatives are chosen by lot from the electorate, then opportunists and zealots cannot use this position to gain power. Of course, morally flawed representatives may be still be drawn by lot, in the same proportion, as there are morally flawed people in the public. Fortunately, immoral people are a usually small minority, and after all, they too have a right for fair representation. This is not any worse than in the representative system, as there are many flawed representatives by the traditional means.

If selection by lot produces representatives who do not fulfil the Direct Democracy Pledge or commit offences while in office, they can be removed by the usual Parliamentary/Congressional procedures. And since they were chosen by lot, their behavior does not reflect on the Direct Democracy movement. Their temporary presence would be understood to be part of the fair process of public representation

How will this system function? In a system with Proportional Representation, the Direct Democracy Party will draw a lot among the list of voters. The chosen candidates would then be offered a place on the Party List in the next election, with a realistic chance to become representatives in the next Parliament.

The citizens chosen by lot would have to agree to serve in Parliament. Since this is an honor with various benefits, such as salary and public visibility, most chosen candidates will probably agree to serve.

Once candidates agreed to be considered, they would undergo a series of tests to prove basic competency. Requirements for representatives should be fair and not exclusionary, but may exclude individuals with, at least recent, criminal records. There may be also a requirement for candidates to have adequate levels of literacy and general knowledge necessary to function in Parliament.

Qualified candidates would then undergo training in parliamentary procedure and the law. For example, they may be tutored by lawyers and by current Direct Democracy Members of Parliament. Working with the current representatives, they would be educated in how to poll their electorate and how to work with Citizen Panels to interpret the public will. They may be also tutored in the fields of various Parliament Expert Agencies such as Budget, Health, Justice, Defense etc. according to their chosen interests. After receiving this education, Direct Democracy Candidates would probably be better qualified to serve in Parliament than current freshmen representatives who often have few skills other than running a campaign.

To maintain continuity and skill, a fraction, perhaps 10%, of the current Direct Democracy delegation would be placed at the top of the Party List to assure a place in the next Parliament. In this manner a proportion of the delegation in Parliament will always be experienced in interpreting and promoting the public will.

Similarly, Representatives for District or Electorate seats in area-based systems can be chosen from the list of eligible voters in the District. These candidates would also be tested for integrity and competence, and educated prior to service similarly to the members of Direct Democracy Party delegation. Of course it must always be emphasized that these citizens are running for election not for themselves but strictly as qualified, but randomly chosen, members of the public.

As to public appeal, the fairness of this system which brings regular people, rather than privileged politicians into Parliament, will appeal to many voters. As well, a real chance to be elected to Parliament may also appeal to many people.

The name "Direct Democracy Party" may sound somewhat radical. Maybe more popular would be a party called "Everyone For Real Democracy". The motto of the Everyone Party may be " Everyone deserves fair representation - and everyone deserves a fair chance to represent the public in Parliament. You too deserve a chance to be in Parliament. "

It is possible that people may think that randomly chosen representatives will not be competent. There is also an ambiguity in the public mind about politicians. On the one hand people criticize and distrust their leaders, and on the other hand people need the faith that they are being lead with competence. It is surprising that the President of the United States or even Prime Ministers are considered as ordinary humans one day before the elections, and are ignored next day if they lose. But if the same people win, the next day they are entrusted with the destiny of the world and are treated with awe as if they are suddenly endowed with superhuman powers.

This ambiguous faith in leaders will make the choice of Representatives by lot hard to accept at first by the public. However, if we believe in the collective wisdom of the people, we must also trust that most of these Representatives will prove at least as competent and honest as others who are chosen through political intrigue. Once this is proven by experience, this attitude will not be an obstacle. Rather, the competence of these Citizen Representatives will itself be a proof of the merits of Direct Democracy.

9. Leadership

In a democracy, the public will, will ultimately prevail. Therefore in the long run, shaping the public will is a more effective form leadership than passing unpopular laws.

Although Representatives are often leading public figures with influential views, if they follow the principles of Direct Democracy, they would not and could not impose their ideas on the public, they lead by advocating new ideas and stimulating debate.

New bills can be initiated by Representatives or by public request as described previously, and submitted to electorate-wide polls. If approved by the public, the bills are then introduced into Parliament or Congress. The Representative will become a leader in government by introducing and promoting these bills for legislation.

Direct Democracy Representatives offer the benefits of both direct and representative democracy. The public can exert true influence by deciding directly on major issues and setting policy guidelines and Representatives can also use their judgement on how to implement the public will in detail when dealing in the daily acts of government.

Trial sample runs on a Direct Democracy platform for Congress in the United States, and for Parliament in New Zealand, were undertaken. The experience showed favorable public reaction, but these trial efforts lacked resources for realistic campaigning. Summary accounts of these experiences, and sample campaign materials that could be useful for future candidates, are described in Appendix 2 Campaign Materials for Direct Democracy Candidates.

Chapter 10
Transition from the Representative System

The transition to Direct Democracy must be done prudently since governments profoundly affect the lives of its people. The transition must be gradual and peaceful, and reversible at all stages should unexpected problems surface.

Probably the easiest way for the transition to occur will be through the election of Direct Democracy Representatives or Parties as described in the preceding chapters. This, if need be, can be reversed simply by once again electing traditional Representatives.

If this transition starts with the election of serious Direct Democracy candidates or parties for Congress or Parliament, their innovative programs will soon attract much attention. They may fair best in liberal-minded urban areas or in strongly independent-minded rural areas or anywhere people see that the representative system has failed by denying them true input into the decision-making process.

Once the first Direct Democracy candidates are elected to Congress or Parliament, their actions will probably be subject to worldwide attention. Direct Democracy Representatives should always be popular since by the very nature of their Direct Democracy program, they will have the support of the majority of their constituents. This experience will be a model for further Direct Democracy Representatives and attract others to become Direct Democracy candidates.

As the movement grows and as the number of Direct Democracy Representatives in Congress or Parliament increases, it will be easier to introduce more Direct Democracy measures, such as public initiatives, referendums and public policy committees adjunct to government departments into the system. Eventually, Direct Democracy Representatives or Parties will win a majority in Congress or Parliament. It will then be possible to gradually introduce institutions that can evolve into the ultimate Direct Democracy institutions: the National Proposal Bank, the Debates Agency, the Referendum and Poll Agency, the Public Ombudsmen and the Policy Juries.

At first these institutions may function together with Congress and Parliament as consulting bodies. For example, the National Proposal Bank may decide to select only those proposals for referendums that have a very high level of demand (perhaps 10 percent of the electorate) with only one or two referendums being allowed in a year. These will be prepared and debated by the Debates Agency with referendums and polls being conducted in the same way they would be held in the ultimate model system. The results may not be initially binding on Congress or Parliament, although a measure supported by a large majority of the voters will be hard to oppose. In this manner, major elements of the Direct Democracy model can be tried out before a complete transition to the ultimate system is made.

Artist's concept of the interior of a space colony. A future community where independent groups will establish new forms of government. These new communities, housing from thousands to millions, can start from the outset to make communal decisions through Direct Democracy.

The Direct Democracy model may also evolve by gradually introducing more initiatives and referendums, and Voters Panels adjunct to the Government Agencies or Ministries, as describes in the chapter on Hybrid Systems.

Direct Democracy may be particularly easy to introduce in new pioneering societies. For example, the social systems of the Israeli Kibbutz settlements, which developed under pioneering conditions, are based on collective decision-making. Much of the early American West also functioned under ad-hoc public law. In the future, Direct Democracy will be well suited for the pioneering societies of space colonies. These space settlements, which will be able to accommodate thousands or millions of people, will acquire independence and self-sufficiency and will need to develop new social structures. The colonists will probably tend to be independent-minded, proud and well educated. They will grow up and live in high-technology environments

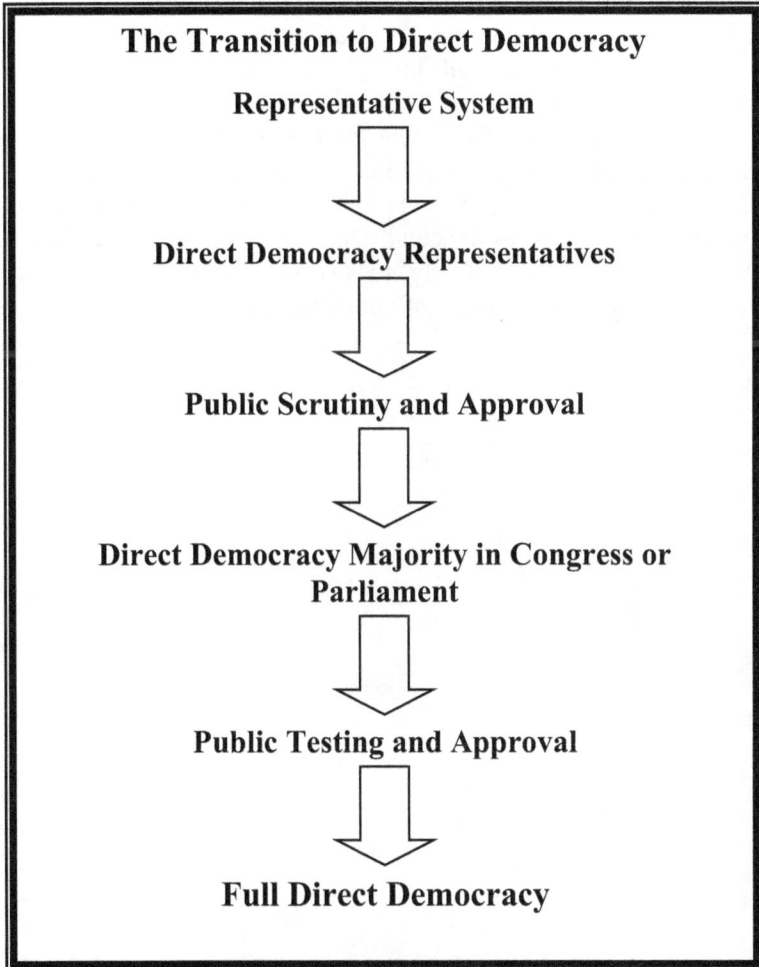

The Transition to Direct Democracy

Representative System

Direct Democracy Representatives

Public Scrutiny and Approval

Direct Democracy Majority in Congress or Parliament

Public Testing and Approval

Full Direct Democracy

with facile communications and computer networks throughout each colony. These conditions will be extremely conducive to communal self-government. Since these new communities will have to start their own form of government without the hindrance of entrenched and outdated traditions, it will be particularly easy to choose Direct Democracy from the outset.

Even with the faults of existing representative systems, there is an increased emergence of democracy worldwide. A basic reason for this may be the revolution in communications where radio, television and computers are available to almost everyone. This technology facilitates public participation as advocated by pioneers of Tele-democracy such as Professor Ted Becker. In times when the minds of people cannot be controlled, their fates cannot be controlled either. It may be the natural outcome of these developments that governments will develop into the form that best suits the majority of people, possibly including global cooperation through a world federation or world government. An educated public can achieve as much direct self-government as it desires to actually handle. Given the natural caution of people, this system is likely to evolve gradually, peacefully and prudently under the guidance of public participation.

Part VI
Features of Direct Democracy

Chapter 11
Leadership

L eaders should direct society with wisdom and vision. However, individuals who achieve power are usually driven by excessive egos and power-lust which are not conducive to enlightened leadership. Although the general public often tends to express their desire for "strong leaders", recent history reminds us that some of the strongest leaders were Hitler, Stalin and Mao Zedong. Most people wouldn't want such personalities to lead them. In contrast, moral leaders are usually outside the power structure and tend to clash with it. Moral leaders such as Moses, Jesus, Gandhi and Martin Luther King all had to struggle against the centers of power. Their ideals were realized only at the cost of much strife and suffering. Direct Democracy would allow the peaceful evolution of new social ideas.

The dangers of individual leadership. Joseph Stalin started as a popular leader, but in the end created a murderous dictatorship.

Visionary leadership can sometimes be beneficial, but even this may be dangerous. To realize their goals, leaders must force people to conform to their vision. In complex societies, even good ideals may have bad consequences. This happens because even benevolent leaders cannot comprehend the full complexities of reality, and try to force society in unnatural directions. This generates opposition, and the system responds by oppression. In the end, the ideals become corrupted and oppression becomes self-serving. Noble ideals were so abused by the Spanish Inquisition that abused religion, and by the oppression that corrupted the communist ideals of social justice. At the end, natural social progress reasserts itself, but at heavy costs. Direct Democracy will prevent such abuses since it will decentralizing decisions and prevent extremists from assuming power.

Social progress can happen through natural social evolution and does not require centralized leadership. In the last decades, great progress has been made in human rights, social services and rights of the disabled. This progress came mostly through enlightened public conscience rather than the acts of powerful leaders. Such progress is due to individuals who exert intellectual, social and cultural rather than political leadership. This is facilitated most readily in free democratic environments that are best secured by Direct Democracy.

Leadership identifies the needed direction of progress. It finds out what actions are needed for this progress, defines and chooses the alternatives, and implements the needed action. Our model system describes how the public could accomplish this through Direct Democracy. The public proposals in the Direct Democracy model provide a ready outlet for new ideas originating from all of society, and with more thinkers, more original ideas will emerge. These ideas will develop further during the Debates, and be implemented into law by decisions made through referendums, polls and Policy Juries.

Leadership by spontaneous ideas from the public is similar to natural evolution. Evolution, which produced all the progress of Life, occurred not in the pursuit of a predefined goal, but rather by spontaneous variations in a broad population, and the natural selection of the viable new forms. Ideas have a life of their own and can evolve in the same manner. When a variety of ideas are allowed to arise and compete, the most viable ones will survive and produce progress. The ideas are tested by reality and progress accordingly. This is better than individual leadership, since no finite human wisdom can compare with the fullness of reality. It is better to allow ideas to arise and develop under the test of survival, than to rely on the limited vision of individual leaders.

Progress that originates from, and that is approved by the majority of the public, will necessarily be popular and therefore enduring. Such progress will be peaceful.

In summary, individual leaders often originate extreme ideas and enforce them through oppression. In contrast, Direct Democracy will allow new ideas to emerge from the larger pool, test them by reality, and allow them to evolve through peacefully natural progress.

Chapter 12
The Rights of Minorities

B ecause Direct Democracy is government by majority vote, it raises the question about the rights of minorities. Of course the need to protect minorities arises in any system. The question raised here is whether minorities will fare better or worse in a Direct Democracy system than under autocracy or representative democracy.

The oppression of minorities would run against the very nature of Direct Democracy. It is unlikely that a society that adopts the liberal principles of Direct Democracy would apply tyranny against the minority groups in its midst. Indeed, Direct Democracy is predicated on faith in the benevolent nature of the collective human will and on dignity that opposes the rule of one person over another. When Direct Democracy is adopted, it will be by a public that strongly believes in these principles. Oppressing minorities would be in contrast to the fundamental values of such a society.

Indeed, in any decent democracy, everyone understands that their freedom and dignity are protected when the rights of all are protected. Trying to oppress anyone would ultimately endanger everyone's own safety. This is a strong motivation against oppressive legislation.

Of course there will always be elements in society who would oppress minorities. These elements are usually extremist segments of a racial or religious minority and are often not representative of the majority. It is important to realize that in Direct Democracy, oppression of minorities would only result if the extremists, along with the cooperation of the majority of people in the nation, vote for such measures. This is unlikely to happen in a true democracy.

Indeed, there appears to be no precedent where any measure of oppression was passed by a referendum vote by the general public. On the contrary, a significant precedent is found in the approval of voting rights for aborigines in Australia. A Constitutional Referendum gave this minority group the right to vote by a 78% margin of votes by the majority white population.

In history, persecution of minorities usually originates from leaders or zealots who needed scapegoats on which to focus public dissent. Even in Nazi Germany and Stalinist Russia, where the population could be brainwashed at will, genocidal atrocities were committed in secret and away from public view. Even in those societies, the leaders realized that such excesses would have generated public revulsion. Such atrocities are much less likely in an open democracy where the natural respect for human life of the majority of people can be expressed freely. Indeed, it is unlikely that abuses could happen in Direct Democracy since the voter would have to assume direct moral responsibility for atrocities committed by the state.

Abuses of minorities can be ranked in seriousness in increasing order starting with social unacceptance, economic discrimination, curtailment of legal rights and educational opportunities, confinement to ghettos, slavery, physical violence and genocide. To the credit of most democracies, the public or the official law has never sanctioned physical violence and genocide against minorities. This fact, and the secrecy in which even the worst dictators have had to conduct their atrocities, is evidence for the fundamental respect for life by the majority of the people.

Of course, no system can inherently guarantee freedom from discrimination. Slavery existed in the original democracies of ancient Greece, in the American democracy before the Civil War and in more modern times the elected governments of South Africa have enforced discrimination through their system of apartheid. Lesser forms of discrimination exist in many democracies. On the other hand, some exceptional autocracies such as the Hapsburg Monarchy, some South American dictatorships and communist governments were liberal toward minorities.

Unavoidably in any system, the fate of minorities always depends on the good will of the majority. As a general rule, the record of democracies on human rights is good. Indeed, many think of democracy and human rights to be synonymous. The more truly democratic societies become, the more dignified and protected we will all be from abuse by the authorities.

The very principles of Direct Democracy rest on freedom and dignity. A society founded on these values is the one most likely to safeguard the freedom and dignity of all of its members.

Chapter 13
Symbols of Power

A ll societies use symbols of power to express group identity and group pride. Usually, leaders become the symbols of the State, and when the State is honored it is often honored through its leaders. In this manner, leaders in conventional governments appropriate the dignities that should belong to all of its citizens. Dictators, Presidents and Prime Ministers are surrounded by ritual and extravagant pomp, which attracts egotists to such positions and fuels their desire for power.

In Direct Democracy the symbols of power should clearly demonstrate that power is vested directly in the people. In Direct Democracy there are no individual dignitaries and every citizen carries the dignity of society. Furthermore, denying the symbols of power to individuals removes a major cause of the greed for power.

Powerful elitist individuals and groups have no place in Direct Democracy. Titles such as "Honorable" and "Excellency" belong to everyone, or to no one. It is important that high officials such as the Heads of Expert Agencies, the Public Ombudsmen and Court Justices should not be addressed by titles lest they themselves and the public come to believe that they deserve special status and power as individuals.

In Direct Democracy every citizen must have an equal chance to represent the state. When ordinary citizens represent the state, it increases the sense of power and participation of all of its citizens.

In the Direct Democracy model, the position of a ceremonial Representative of State for specific occasions will be selected by random from the public. Before officiating, the candidates will be screened by the Ceremonial Committee to be sure that they can function in an appropriately dignified manner. This screening will be free of considerations of wealth, formal education, race, age (except children), sex and state of health and disability (unless this interferes with the required functions). The Representative of State will be instructed in the appropriate rules of protocol and will function at occasions such as state visits, diplomatic receptions, award presentations, parades, cultural opening events, the laying of cornerstones and launchings, signing of laws and other special occasions that are usually attended by dignitaries. Representatives of

State will also deliver television presentations of important government messages to the public.

This position of Representative of State will rotate frequently in order to allow many citizens to share these dignities. A citizen may serve as a Representative of State only for a prescribed period of time, perhaps a few months. There may be as many ceremonial Representatives of State at any time as are needed. Any one Representative of State may officiate at only one event of major significance during their term in office.

Professional speechwriters will prepare the speeches delivered by the Representatives of State. Speeches of national and international significance will have to be vetted and approved in advance by the Executive Council, and of course, they are not allowed to contain any new policy announcements that have not been approved by the public through the usual mechanisms.

For example, a Representative of State who is an average citizen will receive visiting foreign Dignitaries at State House. The Ceremonial Representative of State will deliver the appropriate speeches and will be the personal host of visitors at official receptions and banquets. Representatives of State will fulfil all the functions ordinarily required by state dignitaries including the acceptance of gifts in the name of the state. Representatives of State will deliver summary statements about the matters that were negotiated with the foreign dignitaries during their visits to the appropriate Expert Agencies.

Conversely, when a State Delegation visits another nation, it will be headed by a Representative of State who will receive all the usual honors allotted to dignitaries on such occasions.

At all functions and in any speech, Representatives of State must always emphasize that they are acting on behalf of the entire public.

Of course, Representatives of State will remain ordinary citizens throughout their short service, and will have no individual power whatsoever. Every citizen will have the opportunity to have their name drawn by lot to be selected for this service and to share the dignities of status for a short time. The public will see ordinary citizens such as themselves in positions that symbolize power, and this will inspire a real sense of actually having a share in the communal power.

Material symbols of the powers of the State, such as the design of the flag, national anthem, and the designs of major symbolic state buildings such as the House of Parliament, will be subject to approval by referendum.

Chapter 14
Flexibility and Stability

L ife is a *process* enacted by organic chemical structures. The characteristic feature of a process is ongoing change; therefore life in its diverse manifestations includes continuing change. This is reflected of course in evolution, biological as well as social. The pace of change is especially fast today, driven by technology. The 20th Century saw larger events, World Wars, the rise and fall of Nazism and Communism; and more profound changes: environment, economy, computers, nuclear power, surrogate motherhood, cloning, longevity, space exploration, women's' rights, surge in population - than the preceding Millennia. Great events and profound changes are bound to continue.

As society and its values change, so must its laws and institutions. The Constitution of Direct Democracy must therefore be amenable to change. In the first place, the requirements for Constitutional changes themselves must be subject to evolution by amendments.

The need for flexibility is illustrated by current problems in American society caused by high barriers to Constitutional amendments. For example, with the best of intentions, the Constitution guarantees the freedom of speech and the right to bear arms. Americans are proud of these freedoms.

Yet at the same time, Americans have become *enslaved by freedom*. The freedom of speech, so central to democracy, nevertheless lies at the heart of political corruption in the form of campaign contributions. Because of the Constitutional freedom of speech, the extent of political campaigns in effect cannot be controlled. This requires large expenses for advertising, millions for a seat in the House and up to tens of millions of dollars now for a Senate seat. In the end, the lobbying power of special interests - tobacco, the gun lobby - holds power against the majority will because of the inflexible Constitutional freedom of speech. Due to these powers, guns and shootings are rampant. Certainly two centuries ago the Right to Bear Arms was not intended for schoolchildren to kill each other in play-yards, but this is what an inflexible Constitution lead to.

On the other hand of course, constitutional changes must not be too easy. Stability and long-range planning require a legal framework that is solid and reliable for decades. The Constitution of Direct Democracy provides for constitutional changes with reasonable barriers. As with other aspects of the system, this most basic aspect of the Constitution will itself evolve subject to experience and the public will.

Chapter 15
Peace

L eaders think in terms of national interests, pride, social ideals and geopolitics. In these abstract terms wars may appear as a logical necessity for the resolution of nationalistic goals. The human suffering involved is but an unfortunate detail rarely calculated into the formula.

People think in terms of sustenance, a safe life, a home and the future of their children. In these real terms war is a fearful threat, and especially so is the all-devastating nuclear war.

It is because of the differences between the abstract world of ideologists and leaders, and the real world of people that Direct Democracy offers the best hope for peace.

In fact, the record of democracies on peace is better than that of autocracies. Since the advent of modern democracies, no major war has been started by a democratic government, and all the major wars were started by autocracies. Some local wars were initiated by democracies in response to provocation by autocratic governments. There appears to have been no war in modern history between two democratic nations. Of course, there is no record of Direct Democracies on this issue, but Switzerland, the one nation whose system comes closest to public government, is known for its neutrality and has not been involved in a war since its initiatives and referendum system has been in effect.

Incidentally, the absurdity of war is shown by recent history. In the conflict between communism and capitalism, governments built stockpiles of nuclear arsenals for absurd levels of overkill. In the end, the conflict ended and communism and capitalism merged peacefully. In fact, the communist ideal of the workers owning the means of production is becoming fulfilled through capitalism, as many workers now own shares in manufacturing corporations through stock-market investments. Much before the end of the cold war, the masses of people sensed the injustice of risking all Life for political ideology. The public consistently chose a nuclear freeze and the elimination of nuclear weapons when presented with referendums. If a worldwide referendum was held on nuclear weapons, the vote would most likely abolish nuclear weapons by a large margin.

The abhorrence of nuclear war that was demonstrated in these public votes reflects the deepest human instincts for survival and the continuation of Life. Indeed, nuclear war threatens Life itself. But Life is unique in the universe and the future of Life is limitless. A threat to that future for passing political reasons is unacceptable to the conscience of most people.

At these critical times mass weapons can threaten the lives of millions of people as well as the continuation of the human species and of Life itself. This technology and their weapons are likely to be with us indefinitely. Survival then depends on adjusting our ethics and the institutions that govern society to the presence of this technology. New institutions must be those that best reflect the shared desire for survival. This common instinct is most securely translated into policy through Direct Democracy.

The choice between war and peace should not be deposited with a few narrow-minded ideologists and power-hungry leaders. Rather, the choice should be governed by the common will of people whose primary impulse is the quest for survival.

Chapter 16
World Direct Democracy

"On every level, decisions should be made by those, and only by those, who are affected by the outcome". By this principle, Direct Democracy should govern local, national and global policies where those affected on any level, and only those people, participate in the decision making.

Applied on a global scale, these principles mean that policies that affect all of humanity should be made by all people worldwide, in a World Direct Democracy. This is true even if the groups or territories affected are within the territory of one nation, if the outcome of the policies affects the global community. On the other hand, a World Direct Democracy should not interfere with local or national decisions that affects mainly these groups internally and have no significant affect on others. In fact, an important task of World Direct Democracy is to prevent any group from imposing its will on others. In this manner, a World Direct democracy gives all the self-determination and the independence required for human dignity.

The structure proposed in the Constitution of Direct Democracy can be adapted for a World Direct Democracy with appropriate modifications for the global scale. Concerning a World Direct Democracy, the following questions must be addressed:

1. Is a World Government in general, and a World Direct Democracy in particular, desirable?
2. Is a World Direct Democracy practicable?
3. What would be the authority of a World Direct Democracy? What issues would it govern, and what would be outside its jurisdiction?
4. How would governmental jurisdiction divide amongst the World, regional, national and local governments?
5. How would a World Direct Democracy function?
6. How can a World Direct Democracy be achieved?

16.1 Is a World Direct Democracy Desirable?

After two devastating World Wars and a tense global cold war, the idea of world peace guaranteed by a democratic World Government is attractive. Even after the lessons of these disasters, in the last fifty years there still occurred dozens of wars and incidents of genocide which could have been prevented by an effective World Government. In many cases, Mozambique, Sudan, Kosovo, Bosnia, Rwanda and East Timor, many thousands were killed in civil wars while world diplomats wrangled. Similarly, world help after natural disasters is often delayed due to international indecision.

International tensions and arms races waste great resources. It is most likely that the majority of people in a World Direct Democracy would vote for peace and progress rather than for more war and suffering. A World Direct Democracy is likely to facilitate international disarmament. The resources wasted can be then invested to face common problems, to fight disease, hunger, crime and pollution, natural disasters, for promoting education and research, for protecting biodiversity, developing new resources, for protecting human rights, for the human expansion in space, and for debating and directing genetic engineering.

The technologies emerging now will affect our shared human survival and the basic directions of the human future. It is the moral right of all to shape these decisions. As well, the basic interests of human survival will be best protected by the joint decisions of all of humanity, which distil the common basic human interests from the diverse interest of billions of people.

To establish a World Democracy it is important that every individual human being should be allowed to decide which group or nation to belong to. This should not be a matter of accident of birth.

The only fair and dignified way is to treat every human being as a distinct individual who is judged on his or her own merits. A World Direct Democracy will consider every human being as a citizen of the world community with equal rights to affect the shared human destiny.

16.2. Is a World Direct Democracy Practicable?

First, is a World Government of any form practicable? Can a global society of six billion people, and ten billion in a few decades, be governed by a single government? In fact, the scale of such a government is not exceeding greater than others already in existence. China and India, with populations of a billion, and the United States, Brazil and Russia with continent-sized territories and ethnically diverse populations, are each subject to central governments. In comparison, a World Government needs to be scaled up by only a factor of 5 - 10, which is feasible using the new technologies of communications and data processing.

There already exists a trend toward globalization. Many multinational corporations and direct-sales organizations have branches on every continent. Major regional trade cooperatives and the World Trade Organization manage international commerce. The European Union is undergoing the transition from independent countries to a federation with common laws and currency. In fact, the European Union is a good model where common laws govern areas of shared interest while nations still retain their independence. In principle, this Union could keep expanding until it grows into a World Union.

Global information networks needed for a World Democracy already exist. Important news events are broadcast live on television worldwide. There are international news channels with global coverage and worldwide weather forecasts, and even television talkback shows have worldwide participants. The Internet makes international communication easy, fast and affordable. A person anywhere in the world can access any other person instantaneously through telephone or fax. Internet based chat rooms and e-mail have created a global communication network not even dreamt about a generation ago. Unofficially but in practice, English is becoming a global international language.

The communication technologies are growing rapidly, becoming cheaper and penetrating the developing nations. Over 50% of the people in the US have Internet access, and the number of computer users and internet users worldwide is increasing rapidly. The technology for a World Democracy is likely to be ready much sooner than the political framework.

The United Nations is a constructive step toward a World Government. The UN has made significant contributions in peacekeeping and in promoting human rights, health, food and culture worldwide. Unfortunately, the UN falls short of what a World Democracy could accomplish. The UN is composed of representatives of States, some of them undemocratic, some token democracies, and various representative democracies, none of which empower individual citizens. As well, small and large nations have equal voting rights in the General Assembly, which prevents proportional representation of the world's people. The Security Council is controlled by the major powers and disenfranchises smaller nations. The UN may be the best international forum presently, but it does not satisfy morally or in its powers the roles of a World Direct Democracy.

16.3 The Jurisdiction of a World Direct Democracy

What should be the powers and limits of a World Direct Democracy? This most basic question should be decided by global referendums.

There are issues that affect every human being in the present, or that will have global consequences in the future. The legacy that we leave is likely to affect everyone's descendants as the human genetic pool keeps mixing through the generations. The issues that affect every human being or our shared descendants should be controlled by all the human community.

a. International Peace and Human Rights

Today local conflicts have global consequences. Local wars can draw in others from the region. International and inter-group conflicts spawn international terrorism. Mass weapons are becoming more common and local conflicts can general nuclear and biological warfare with world-wide consequences. Human rights violations anywhere set bad precedents. In a world where human rights can be abused, no one is safe. Because war, peace and human rights affect everyone, these matters should be controlled by the global community. World Democracy can maintain an international emergency force that is ready to intervene when military buildup threatens peace or persecutions and genocide are starting.

World Democracy can have an elected Emergency Manager to authorize rapid deployment. As well, it is possible to conduct a representative emergency global Poll of say 100,000 randomly chosen respondents worldwide to authorize such interventions. The list of Poll Respondents can be maintained and updated permanently and can be ready for use anytime.

The respondents would be contacted by e-mail, fax or telephone sent material with background information and given contact addresses for further information. After two days of studying and discussing the materials, the respondents can send in their vote whether they authorize the intervention. Details such the use of force and lethal force, where and how long the force is permitted to stay and what should it accomplish, can be also decided by this or subsequent Polls. The votes can be counted in real time by computers.

Democratic global decisions about peacekeeping can be made and implemented in days, while the conflict is still limited and before much damage has been done. Months of wrangling by diplomats and governments while thousands are killed are an abomination and are no longer needed. Peace-keeping actions and calls for peace negotiations that have been decided democratically by the global community will also carry great moral authority.

In terms of human rights, this is the ideal role of a World Democracy Government. Ideally, every ethnic, religious and national group should have the right to live as they choose, and to control their members to the extent that they see right. Every individual should have the right to belong to any group and to accept its laws, or not to belong to the group. No person should be forced to live or behave against their own free will and conscience.

b. The Environment
    Nature consists of interacting ecosystems, while national borders are artificial human constructs. Therefore, many environmental issues are international by nature. Air pollution, the pollution of rivers and oceans, acid rain, over fishing and climate change are all international issues.

The survival of plant and animal species affects the future of Life. Even when a species lives within one nation's borders, it belongs to the total web of life. A nation has the responsibility to assure that its wildlife survives, but it does not have the moral right to exterminate it. A species that survives can evolve and spread to other habitats, maybe, in human hands, even to other worlds. The lines of life that may emerge from any species during future eons are much more profound than short-term economic gains of a group of people that may exterminate them.

It is questionable whether humans have the moral right to decide the survival of species, but in practice, we do have these powers. It should be then at least the right and responsibility of the entire human community to make these life-and-death decisions.

c.   Genetic Engineering

Beyond survival, humans through genetic engineering will also control the future of life. In what direction should humans evolve? What body shapes and sizes, how much intelligence should the next generations have? Which body parts should remain natural and organic, and which should be replaced by mechanical devices and computers? How long should people be designed to live? What are the ultimate objectives in designing these future humans?

These are clearly policies that will profoundly affect the future of all of our descendants for eons. These are also questions that technology will force upon society within decades. It may be beyond human powers to have the necessary wisdom; but at least, those decisions must rely on the deepest human feelings for survival and life. They are clearly not decisions that any human has the right to impose on the descendants of other free humans. Any attempt to do will likely cause terrible wars including mass weapons.

Both the interests of Life and human survival, morality demands that these decisions should be made jointly by all humanity, as provided by a World Direct Democracy.

d.   Space

The future of life is evidently in space. How far can life grow in space? Our Solar System alone can support 10 trillion people, the population of ten thousand worlds. There are 100 billion stars in the Milky Way Galaxy and 100 billion galaxies in the universe.

Who owns the universe? Should individuals, corporations or governments be able to claim space objects and to mine or settle them? If not, on what basis can they be used? Whom can they be leased from?
These questions too will control our shared future. If we want to avoid Evil Empires and Star Wars, these issues too must be decided jointly by all humanity through a World Direct Democracy.

e. What shouldn't a World Government control?
    While global management is needed, it doesn't follow that society
    itself should be homogeneous. A diversity of cultures is enriching
    and many groups take pride in their identities. Diversity and group
    pride demand that every group should live under the laws and
    traditions it prefers. A World Direct Democracy should manage
    only those issues with international implications, such as those
    listed above.

The basic human rights that all people should enjoy should be
defined, monitored and enforced by the global community. On the other
hand, issues of religion, education, detailed moral codes, crime and
punishment, local and national budgets and public services should be
best decided by groups who share common cultural values. These of
course could also be managed best by local Direct Democracy if the
group so desires.

In practice, a World Government could not manage the affairs
of local communities and nations worldwide. In fact, these matters
involve decisions that do not affect people in other communities. The
principle of democracy may be re-stated: *It would be therefore against
the spirit of democracy that decisions on these matters should be made
by people who are not affected.* It would be proper for the global
community to manage those affairs that are international, that extend
across borders or that have clear implications for the whole human
community. Such matters include peacekeeping between groups and
nations, managing global common areas including the international
waters, Antarctica and all of outer space, managing the environment on
all levels since the ecosystems of the world are all connected;
promoting inter-regional communications and trade with the possible
use of a global currency (the Euro is a good model), and also, possibly
promoting education on subjects of shared human interests, such as on
human rights, health, the environment, science, world government, and
the promotion of a world language.

In particular, the regulation of genetic technology should be
through a global authority. It is quite likely that deliberate intervention
with human genetics will become possible now that cloning and
genetically modified organisms have been successfully accomplished
with other species. Once a genetic change is induced anywhere, its
effects will ultimately spread through the entire human gene pool. Such
acts will alter the entire evolutionary future of the human species. This

is a matter that should be governed by the shared decisions of the entire human community.

On the other hand, it would be appropriate for individual communities and nations to manage their own affairs. In any event, it would be impossible for a central world government to manage the affairs of every community in detail. Diverse ethnic and religious groups perceive human issues differently, and want to follow their own traditions and values in these matters. Such issues include civil and criminal affairs, commercial law, local taxes, local and ethnic education, crime control, health systems, social welfare and retirement.

In summary, a World Direct Democracy Government should control the basic issues that effect world peace, human rights, the shared global environment and resources, and basic developments that affect the shared human future. It should guarantee the rights of people to belong to any chosen group or nation. It should mediate in disputes between groups and nations, and prevent any group or nation from imposing its will on others. It should not interfere with the autonomy of any group or nation in matters that don't affect others.

16.4 Institutions and Procedures of a World Direct Democracy

A World Direct Democracy may function similarly to the model system described in the "Constitution of Direct Democracy".

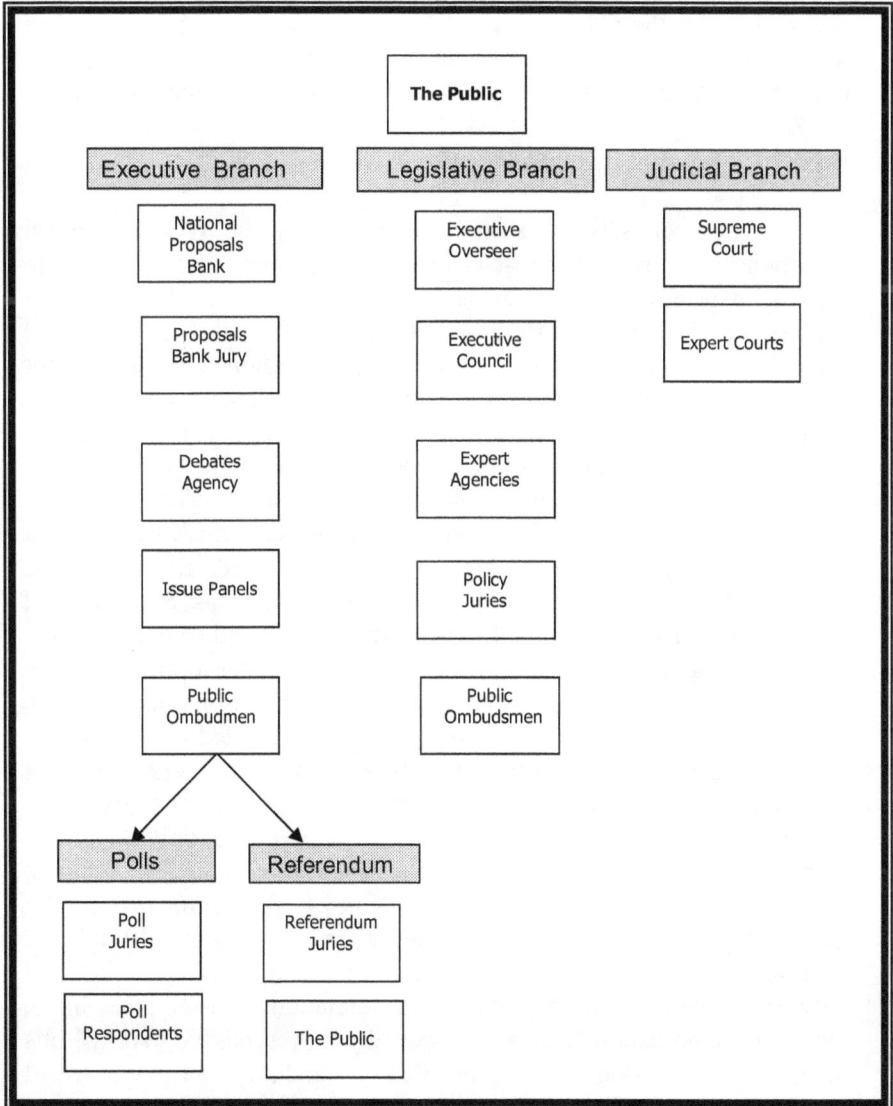

Step 1 - The Public Submits Proposals to the World Proposal Bank

On any level, the first public right to secure is that the policy-making agenda is itself defined by the people, through Citizen Initiated Referendums. In the proposed system this is accomplished by allowing citizens to submit referendum proposals to the World Proposal Bank. Whereas under the Constitution of Direct Democracy each citizen can propose up to three issues a year, on a global scale it may be necessary to limit the number of submissions to one proposal per voter per year.

Step 2 - The World Proposal Bank Manages the Proposals

The proposals are sorted and tallied by the World Proposal Bank whose primarily purpose is to sort the millions of proposals into logical "issue groups". There may be thousands of similar proposals which, though worded differently, would fall into the same general category or theme. For example, there may be millions of proposals for full global disarmament, others to ban all mass weapons, others to ban nuclear weapons or weapons testing, all expressed perhaps in a slightly different manner. The Proposal Bank sorts these into groups and counts the proposals relating to the same issue. The adjunct Proposals Jury then checks the sorting and classifies proposals that are hard to categorize. Because of the large volumes involved, there may be Proposal Juries specializing in various areas such as Security and Disarmament, Human Rights, Environment, Health and so on.

The number of proposals needed to qualify for a referendum or poll would have to be large enough to constitute a reasonable threshold. For example, ten million proposals may be needed for a World Referendum and two million proposals for World Poll. The proposals should also represent the wider international community. For example, of the ten million proposals required for a referendum, only 25% may come from one nation or 50% from one region or continent. Of course, there must be limits on the number of World Referendums that can be held each year. This number is limited by the costs, by the difficulty to educate the world population about the issue, and also by the fact that only basic issues should be subject to referendums. On the other hand, much the same benefit can be achieved by representative World Polls involving say 20,000 respondents chosen randomly from the world population. It is easier to educate Poll Respondents about issues and policy options and to conduct the poll. Whereas World Referendums may be possible only on a few major issues per year, it is possible to manage a much larger number of polls, at least 20 - 40 per year or as required by the public Proposals.

Step 3 - The Debates
- The Debates Agency Organizes the Public Debates
- The Issue Panels Prepare the Debate Materials
- Referendum Jury Supervises the Debates

The Debates Agency has the responsibility of organizing and conducting non-biased and informative worldwide debates. The Debates Agency forms an Issues Panel for each of the proposal issues. The task of the Issues Panel is twofold. First it ensures that the wording of the proposals retains the common content extracted from the millions of related proposals, and that the final wording is clear and unambiguous. Secondly, the Issues Panel prepares the debate material. The proposals and debate material are then translated into all of the agreed upon list of languages. When World Democracy is instituted, much of the world population may use a common language, probably English. Computerized translation between languages should also become possible. A panel of professional translators ensures that the wording of the proposals and debate material is consistent in all languages. Information packs of the debate material are then made available to the world public through newspapers, magazines, television, radio, videos, movie theater advertisements, organized public debates and the ubiquitous Internet. There is already hardly a place on Earth that is isolated from mass communication, and its reach will keep broadening. During the Debate Period, the public (during polls, the Poll Respondents) can get further information from representatives of the Debates Agency and from volunteers and organizations knowledgeable about the issue. Throughout this period, the Referendum Jury supervises the debates to ensure they are conducted in a balanced and non-manipulative manner.

Step 4 -The Vote
- Referendums and
- Polls

The Referendum and Polls Agency conducts the actual voting and ensures that it is free and made available everywhere. As much as possible, voting is done through telephone banks and the Internet. Voting centers may be established worldwide where free voting is assured. Voting is done over a period of several months to ensure that all can cast votes. The results are not disclosed until the end of the voting period. Some nations may incorporate the referendum vote into their national elections, thereby reducing the overall cost.

Polls are votes conducted using a statistical sample of individuals (the Poll Respondents), who are representative of the public rather than all eligible voters. Representative World Polls would require more Poll Respondents than national polls for a sample that truly represents the global community. It would seem that 10,000 - 20,000 people drawn randomly from a global list could make up a sufficient sample. Poll Issue Panels and Poll Juries supervise the selection of Poll Respondents to ensure it is random and unbiased. The tasks of the Poll Issue Panels are similar to those performed by the Issue Panels in preparing for a referendum. They have to identify the issue alternatives, prepare the issue information packs and oversee that their translations into languages on the language list are consistent and unbiased.

Step 5 - Implementation of Policy: The Expert Agencies
   • Policy Juries and Public Ombudsmen Monitor the actions
      of the Expert Agencies

Expert Agencies are administrative departments entrusted with the responsibility of implementing the will of the global community that was previously decided through referendums and polls. Examples of Expert Agencies are the Health Services Expert Agency, the Defense Expert Agency, the Debates Agency and the Commerce Expert Agency. It is important to maintain a balance of representation in a world government, therefore, the heads of each of the Expert Agencies will come from a different country.

Adjunct to each of these agencies is a Policy Jury whose members are chosen by lot from the global population. The role of the Policy Jury is to ensure that the actions of the Expert Agencies directly reflect the will of the people. Policy Jurors receive specialized instruction in the Expert Agency's field of activities, e.g. health, employment, education etc. In order that the juries adequately represent worldwide opinion the number of jurors would have to be greater than the Policy Juries used by national governments.

Because Referendums and Polls can cover only major issues, the main body of detailed public law derives from the decisions of Policy

Juries. If Expert Agencies are unsure of the application of the public law, or no pertinent law currently exists, the Policy Juries can formulate the law. Policy Juries have this authority as they are representative of the public. The Policy Juries can also veto any action of the Expert Agencies they find that is not adhering to the public law and require correction.

World Policy Juries would have to meet periodically until teleconferencing by thousands of people worldwide becomes feasible. Internet chat rooms are a current development in this direction.

In addition to Policy Juries, a committee of five Public Ombudsmen, selected from the global population for their proven expertise in the Expert Agency's area of specialty, is attached to each Expert Agency. The role of the Public Ombudsmen is to ensure that Agencies act according to the established public will. Ombudsmen also arbitrate disputes between the Expert Agencies and their associated Policy Juries, and may suggest corrective action when they find that the Expert Agencies or the Policy Juries are in conflict with the public will. However, Public Ombudsmen cannot formulate new policies and cannot enforce any decisions.

Public Ombudsmen also monitor the referendum and polls processes to ensure that the debate material is fair, unbiased and is available worldwide.

Step 6 - The Executive Council Handles Emergencies that Require Immediate Attention

Situations often arise, especially on a global scale, which require immediate attention. The Executive Council, made up of the heads of the Expert Agencies, is empowered to make emergency decisions without the benefit of a worldwide referendum or poll. The Executive Council must transfer the handling of emergency matters to the appropriate Expert Agency and Policy Jury as promptly as possible.

Step 7 - The Judicial System
* Expert Courts
* The Supreme Court

At the present time most courts and judges may handle cases ranging from family affairs and criminal law to citizenship, banking, environmental issues, industrial patents, copyrights, computer fraud etc.

Clearly, it is beyond the ability of any one individual to make knowledgeable judgements in all of these areas. These shortcomings become acute when the field is highly technical and requires specialized knowledge. Under World Direct Democracy each Expert Court is headed by a team of three Justices who are *expert* in their court's area of specialization in the same manner that the heads of Expert Agencies must show demonstrated expertise in their areas. Justices of the courts are elected publicly. No two of the three Justices in each court may come from the same country.

Decisions of the Expert Courts can be appealed to Expert Panels of the Supreme Court. The panels are composed of emeritus Expert Justices and emeritus Chiefs of Expert Agencies and the Chief Justices of the Expert Courts. Decisions of the Supreme Court can be appealed through proposals for referendums and polls to the ultimate authority, the voting public.

- **Dispute Resolution**

Public policies (i.e., laws) under World Direct Democracy are determined by worldwide referendums and polls. Expert Agencies implement public policies and Policy Juries and Public Ombudsmen monitor the Expert Agencies. When the interpretation and/or implementation of those policies are challenged, there is a formal procedure to resolve the disputes, see the Policy Disputes Resolution Table below.

- **Financing a World Direct Democracy**

The operations of a World Democracy can be supported by a very small individual tax by taxpayers worldwide. There will be just one World Direct Democracy Government and its costs would have to be distributed over the whole world population. Therefore the costs to the individual taxpayer will be small. This tax will be equitable and proportional to income on an absolute basis.

16.5 Building a World Direct Democracy

Evidently, a World Direct Democracy may become a reality at best in many decades. However, there are actions that we can pursue now that will promote this ultimate form of communal global self-determination.

1. Promote Democracy Worldwide in Any Form. Democracy has made great progress in the last decades of the 20th Century. However, still only a fraction of the world's population live in well entrenched, reliable democracies. Many nations are still ruled by dictators and military juntas, one-party hegemony, or token democracies run by rich and powerful elite. Certainly, any form of true democracy is preferable. It is important that people experience democracy and learn the basic principles of democracy: To accept that the opposition may be in power and that to enact change you should fight your opponents with *ballots rather bullets*. Once democracy has been accepted and entrenched, people will want more real power through Direct Democracy. It is of course also easier to transform representative democracies to direct democracies, and democratic governments are more likely to allow citizens to participate in a World Direct Democracy. In fact, if enough voters demand it, democratic governments will have to do so.

2. Build Direct Democracy Locally. There are many groups active in promoting referendums and their use is increasing. There are many means, such as lobbying, Letters to the Editor, talkback shows and internet groups that are already dedicated to Direct Democracy on local and national levels. Much can be done by interested parties through these means.

3. Run for Office as a Direct Democracy Representative. This may be the most efficient way to introduce Direct Democracy into existing systems. The pledge of a Direct Democracy Representative or Party is "On every major issues, I shall vote in Parliament (or Congress) as instructed by the majority vote of my constituents". By this simple device, Direct Democracy can be introduced gradually into any democratic system easily and without changing the structures of the existing system. Direct Democracy Candidates can run for any office, including Members of Parliament, Congressmen, Senators and even Presidents. Even if the first runs are symbolic, they are a great way to publicize the case for Direct Democracy; and there is always a chance that some candidates will actually win! Once in office, they will be watched by the media and if true to their vow, Direct democracy will grow increasingly popular.

4. A Volunteer Direct Democracy World Government. While the establishment of a World Direct Democracy is well into the future, a model body can be constructed at the present time. This body may be first constituted by people currently involved in promoting Direct Democracy, as well as invited and well respected personalities world-wide. The Acting World Direct Democracy Government would be constituted by Expert Panels dedicated to specific areas such as Environment, Human Rights, Disarmament, Crime Prevention, Children Rights, International Resources and Technology Evaluation. Each panel would involve experts representing all the sides of the issues. For example, in the Environment Panel, there will be representatives from environmental organizations (Greenpeace, Friends of Earth, Union of concerned Scientists, National Resources Defense Council and similar organizations world-wide), as well representatives of mining, forestry, energy, chemical and agricultural industries, Governmental and UN Environmental Agencies and academic researchers. These panels could select issues for World-Wide Polls, prepare balanced Debate materials and select and educate a world-wide representative Environmental Policy Jury. They may also conduct worldwide representative polls on selected issues.

The results of these worldwide polls will be sent to all governments and are likely to be reported by the worldwide media. They will have great moral authority, as they will for the first time, fairly represent the public world opinion of all people on important global issues.

The Model World Direct Democracy will show the way to the real system. Eventually, it will accumulate a set of policies preferred by the majority of humanity. It will test the feasibility and strength of the systems, and will reveal any improvements that can develop along the way. Participation would be continually expanded to increasingly reflect the true global opinions. If successful, eventually the world public will demand that its rulings become international law and it will be converted from a symbolic to a real World Direct Democracy Government.

National governments will not willingly give up any portion of their sovereign powers to a World Government. The United Nations is composed of representatives of a world divided into national groups and is continually a battleground of national interests. Conversely, in a World Direct Democracy every human being participates individually. This system does not divide people into arbitrary groups. Because World Direct Democracy diminishes the power of local politicians, they are unlikely to promote it. The initiative will have to come from the people. This will occur naturally when common global problems demand common solutions. The success of Direct Democracy systems locally will help a public move toward Direct Democracy on a global scale.

Before a World Direct Democracy can be organized, there needs to be a focus and an organizing entity. Perhaps the most effective start will be through a volunteer World Government. The members will not be national delegates looking out for the interests of their nations but individuals concerned with the global good. Indeed, it is necessary to have such a trial system in place before real decisions of global significance are entrusted to this new system.

At first, this volunteer body can start as a group of respected experts (retired people would most likely have the time and money needed to participate). They might arrange to meet once a year, debate problems that would be within the jurisdiction of a World Government and recommend policies. Well-reputed international organizations may also choose to participate and give expert advice. Such participating groups could be for example, the International Red Cross, Amnesty International, the World Wildlife Fund, the International Court, the World Bank, Greenpeace, Interpol etc. In fact, an organizing body may ask these organizations to nominate members for the first volunteer World Government. Approval by these organizations will increase the moral authority of the first volunteer World Government. Delegates would serve for a period of four years.

The volunteer World Government would only have moral authority of course. But acting as a World Government, being impartial and being of high reputation, its decisions will be visible worldwide and well respected.

To enhance its authority and to move toward true global democracy, the volunteer World Government will conduct international public opinion polls on major issues. The poll respondents will be selected randomly worldwide. The very existence of such worldwide polls will be noteworthy and have a unifying influence. The volunteer World Government will gain much credibility if it closely follows world opinions. It should indeed, make it their policy based on the results of the worldwide opinion polls. It may call for worldwide referendums on very significant global issues such as nuclear weapons, the status of outer space and Antarctica, measures against greenhouse warming and ozone depletion.

Once the volunteer World Government is active, it should move resolutely to make its procedures as democratic as possible. First, it should seek to become an elected body. Ultimately, the elections for World Government should be open to all people of voting age globally. Until that becomes feasible, the volunteer World Government could develop a support organization with supporters worldwide. Supporting members can then vote to elect the World Government. Membership fees should of course be scaled in various nations to make it affordable everywhere.

The World Government Organization will nominate a list of candidates for each election. The list will be sent to the members of the World Government Supporters Organization worldwide for voting. Referendums, initiatives and polls should also be conducted frequently among the membership to help the World Government formulate popular policies.

It is the very essence of World Government that it should consider the global good in preference to local interests. Therefore the elections should allow no national or religious bias. For this reason the list of candidates will have to be anonymous. For each candidate, a description of their background related to the office: professional education and positions (in general, without specifying the organizations, which may give away their nationality) will be given to the public. For example: Candidate A for Minister of Environment received a university degree in economics; served as a consultant for a forestry company; was director of a government department for natural resources; and served on the board of a conservation organization. The candidates will also disclose and answer questions by the public on their views and plans about issues related to the office.

16.6 Breaking Down National Barriers

The main obstacle to any World Government is the division of the world into separate nations. Indeed, much trouble in history resulted from prejudices that stereotype people according to ethnic and national lines. However, grouping people by nations is highly arbitrary. Many nations are composed of ethnic, religious or economical groups who have little in common with each other but share more with related groups in other countries. National chauvinism, which has caused so much trouble, war and suffering, is nothing but a throwback to prehistoric tribalism deeply ingrained in human nature.

How arbitrary and shallow national divisions are can be seen by many examples. In immigrant nations such as the US and Australia, national identities usually last only a few, often one or two generations (religious and especially racial divisions last longer). Americans from all origins assume American patriotism often in one generation, even people from nations hostile to each other. Of course, many Americans of German and Italian origins fought bravely against Germany and Italy in the World Wars, along with Americans of British, French, Russian and many other origins. As well, nations that were deadly enemies within the lifetime of a still living generation, such as Germany, Italy, the UK and France are now united in friendship in the European Union. Often soldiers killing each other on opposing sides reunite in friendships a few decades after a battle.

These examples show that the division of people by nationality is arbitrary and meaningless. A French, Portuguese, Argentine or Polish musician, artist, scientist or businessman is likely to have more in common with each other than with their compatriots of a different character and education living across town. Many people have personal enemies at work or as neighbors but friendly colleagues worldwide.

Fortunately, these arbitrary national groupings are breaking down with international travel, conferences, regional unions, internet communications, common science and technologies, a practical common language, common dress fashions, common foods, a common culture of popular music and movies. After a few generations grow up in this interlinked world, a World Direct Democracy will look increasingly, as the best way to manage the common human interests.

Can the Public Judge Complex Issues?

"It is evident that the proposed Debates can educate the public sufficiently if each voter studies each referendum issue for at least one hour. It is a major task of the system to achieve this much public motivation."

Chapter 17
Can the Public Judge Complex Issues?

Many important issues require basic judgements about ethical and/or economic priorities: abortion, criminal justice, war/peace, environmental protection, social welfare, fair taxation, civil rights and human rights. Many issues are complex and technical with factual knowledge being essential in making meaningful choices. Can the lay public handle such issues?

First, we observe that representative democracy also leaves decision-making to laymen. The President or Prime Minister is often a person whose main experience is in political intrigue and campaign posturing. Among the recent American Presidents were ex-lawyers, ex-businessmen, an actor and a naval officer. Other Prime Ministers, Congressmen and Members of Parliament have similar lay backgrounds. These people are then called upon to be Commanders-in-Chief of high technology armies; decide on complex international trade agreements, public health, tax laws, monetary and fiscal policy, environmental regulation and nature conservation, global diplomacy, arms control of complex weapons systems - all at the same time. It is humanly impossible even for a highly learned person to have a general understanding of all of these fields, much less for politicians who must dedicate most of their to political maneuvering.

It may be preferable to leave all decisions to experts, but this is not consistent with real democracy. In the proposed model system Policy Juries present a compromise solution. Policy Juries are selected from the general public and the number of members of each jury is large enough to be a representative cross-section of the public. Each juror would receive education and experience for a year in a given field before becoming a voting member. This would provide a level of specialized knowledge appropriate for making reasoned decisions.

Even so, can a large group of lay people such as the proposed Policy Juries be sufficiently educated to make learned decisions? This question was thoroughly investigated by The Public Agenda Foundation based in New York. Their approach was to assemble focus groups or panels that represented a cross-section of the voting age population. Focus groups dealt with for example, environmental issues, criminal justice, and the public school system.

A representative study by the Public Agenda Foundation dealt with two issues, solid waste disposal and the greenhouse effect. The 402 participants first completed a questionnaire that measured their understanding of the issues and their preferences about solutions. Next, they watched and discussed informative videos that presented the general problem and the merits and disadvantages of alternative solutions along with scientific disagreements on these problems. Finally, the participants completed the questionnaire again. The Public Agenda Foundation also conducted similar sessions with over 400 scientists, not experts, but people trained in the analytical approach to risk-benefit evaluation, uncertainties, and the nature of theories and hypotheses.

In other studies on criminal punishment, participants were asked for their "gut reaction" to questions such as: "should criminals be sentenced to severe jail sentences, or handled by alternative methods, such as community work and restitution to the victims?" Usually, the gut reaction reflected the general uneducated lay public opinion. The focus groups were then presented with additional data, such as the costs of jail, statistics of repeat offending, overcrowding and rehabilitation. Usually, when the participants realized that simplistic gut responses were inadequate, considered reflections then gained ground.

The main finding was that the views of the lay participants, after the brief educational exposure, were closely similar to the scientifically trained group exposed to the same information. The analysts of the Public Agenda Foundation derived the following conclusions from these studies:

1. The general public can thoughtfully judge complex scientific issues given relatively brief and specific information about them.
2. The public does not require extensive scientific knowledge to thoughtfully consider complex scientific issues. However, a framework of real-life choices with benefits and risks is instrumental for the public to assess the issues.
3. The public does not expect science to deliver magical risk-free solutions.
4. The public is not paralyzed by scientific uncertainty.

The experience with the public panels lead Daniel Yankelovich, a director of Public Agenda Foundation to distinguish between "public opinion" and "public judgement". The former is the public viewpoint that may be vague, confused and emotional. The latter is the public viewpoint after serious consideration over an extended period of time.

These studies by the Public Agenda Foundation have direct relevance to the proposed Direct Democracy model. First, it is evident that the proposed Debates can educate the public sufficiently if each voter studies each referendum issue for at least one hour. It is a major task of the system to achieve this much public motivation.

The proposed Policy Juries will make the most important contribution to the Direct Democracy system. The jurors, with years of service in a specific policy area, would have ample opportunity to develop informed judgement. Jurors would generally be better educated and more informed in their specialist areas than current members of Parliaments or Congresses, whose members must vote on all issues, and probably lack extensive knowledge in any one area. At the same time, the jurors will still represent a cross-section of the public, more faithfully than does Congress or Parliament.

Even broader participation can be achieved through Voters Forums. Here all the voters nationwide who are interested in a policy area become educated in that field. To participate, citizens may be required to attend courses either in person, by mail, by tele-education, by the internet, and possibly even being required to pass a qualifying examination. All of these interested and educated citizens are then polled on the main issues in that area. It is fair to say that any person who studies a specific field, such as welfare policy or environmental protection during two weekend seminars and a two-month evening course will be better educated in that field than a Congressman without any training in the area.

In addition, Voters Forums can be combined with the Policy Jury system, where the Juries act on most matters, and refer, say, the top ten percent of important issues to the Voters Forums. Using such methods, complex issues will be decided by well-informed panels who are truly representative of the public, rather than scantly informed politicians who represent only themselves or special interests.

The Public Will

Policy Juries

Referendums

Polls

Informed Debates

Direct Democracy

Chapter 18
Direct Democracy in History and in the Present

Demokratia - The Greek roots of the word demokratia are <u>demo</u> "the people" and <u>kratos</u> "rule".

T he point of the present book is *that all people have an inherent right to participate in decision-making.* Representative Democracy arose when collective action was impractical due to primitive transportation and communication systems, as well as the physical distances between the people and the government. Now that technology has succeeded in creating worldwide communication down to an individual level, the people can now assert their rights to participate in making the decisions that affect their lives.

Ancient Greece
Home of the First Direct Democracies

Direct Democracy was the first form of public government in the city-states of ancient Greece. Athenian democracy was characterized by direct participation of their citizens in the decision-making process of their government. Laws were made by large assemblies of citizens and officials serving on a rotational basis, were selected by lot.

A form of Direct Democracy was practiced in England and the American colonies in the 17th and 18th centuries. The history was described in detail in a recent book entitled "Inventing the People", by Edmund S. Morgan, with numerous references to the historic sources.

Some aspects of this history are of interest in relation to the Direct Democracy Representative proposals in this book, and are briefly reviewed here.

In early England, it was recognized that all people have the inherent right to assemble and legislate. Representation was only a convenience and a necessity since an assembly of the whole populace was impractical. For example, King James I stated to Parliament that since it was impossible "for all the gentlemen and burgesses to be present at every parliament, therefore a certain number is selected...". William Ball stated in 1645 that "if the people without confusion or disorder could assemble together, there were no need of such election (of representatives)".

A portion of the Magna Carta - signed by King John of England in 1215.
A significant step in the transition from monarchy to democracy.

In America, where democracy was reconstituted at a distance from the monarchy, it did start in some places as a direct democracy. Such assemblies of "free men" took place in the state of Maryland. At the Federal Convention of 1787 it was stated that representation was "an expedient by which an assembly of certain individuals chosen by the people substituted in place of the inconvenient meeting of the people themselves". The first Congress asserted that "If it were consistent with the peace and tranquillity of the inhabitants, every freeman would have a right to come and give his vote."

Historic precedents for Direct Democracy Representatives can be found in the types of instructions that boroughs or counties gave to their representatives. This was a common practice in England in the seventeenth century. Such instructions concerned local matters such as instructing representatives to secure some local construction or local tax relief from the central government. In about 1640, the instructions were also related to national religious matters. The number of instructions given to members of the Parliament in Westminster increased during the political crises of the 18th century. The giving of instructions to representatives was also a common practice in some of the America Colonies. For example, the town of Boston issued instructions to its representatives in the Massachusetts Assembly at least 18 times before 1689. New England town hall meetings also issued instructions to their representatives. Indeed, the Massachusetts Constitution of 1780 stated that "The people have the right, in an orderly and peaceable manner, to assemble to consult upon the common good....to give instructions to their representatives." The constitutions of New Hampshire, Vermont, Pennsylvania, and North Carolina also included similar statements.

A most interesting precedent to the proposed Direct Democracy Representatives were events that took place in England in the 18th century. The city of Bristol in 1701 sent an instruction to its representative with the preface that "it is no doubt to us that we have a right to direct our Representatives". Members of the Parliament often replied to such assertions with statements such as "We thankfully acknowledge your commands, and with Joy receive your Renewal of a Fundamental Right." Thomas Gage, a member of the House of Commons from Tewkesbury, stated after an action in 1740 that "I am required so by my constituents, who, I think, have the right to direct those that represent them."

The direct representative pledge proposed in this book was in fact required by the radical Whigs in London and Westminster in 1774. They sought pledges from candidates to obey any instructions given to them.

These incidents of Direct Representation were however, rare. The opposite attitude was formulated most prominently by Edmund Burke. This central argument was that "Parliament is not a Congress of ambassadors from different and hostile interests...but a deliberative assembly of one nation, with one interest, that of the whole. You chose a member, indeed, but when you have chosen him, he is not a member of Bristol, but he is a Member of Parliament." He also stated that "Your

149

representative owes you, not his industry only, but his judgement; and betrays, instead of serving you, if he sacrifices it to your opinion."

The argument that Parliament must serve an entire nation, rather than a locality, is of course valid. To its proponents, it would have seemed inconceivable that issues could be deliberated and voted upon by an entire nation, or even by a global community numbering billions of people. Indeed, a nationwide and global Referendum would, necessarily, reflect the communal rather than local interests. This argument has now turned around to favor, rather than negate, Direct Democracy. And as to representatives substituting their own opinions to that of their constituents, in a true democracy it is that superiority and power that must be taken away from individuals.

More recently, Direct Democracy has been practiced in the cantons of Switzerland from the 19th century, and the country retains the largest measure of direct democracy of all the contemporary nations. First, all changes in the Federal Constitution must be approved in a national Referendum by the majority of votes cast and by the majority of the Swiss cantons. Referendums to change the Constitution may be initiated by the people through a petition by 50,000 voters, or by the legislature. Both may initiate partial or total revisions of the Constitution. Partial revision may be requested in general terms, or the petitioners may propose a specific text. The legislature may then submit the proposal for Referendum, or it can

Switzerland has practiced Direct Democracy since the 19th century. A multicultural society where peace and prosperity reward a government based on public participation.

The village of Zermatt with the Matterhorn in the background.

submit it with a recommendation to reject; or it can submit it along with a counterproposal.

Furthermore, the constitution requires that all federal laws and universally binding "arretes" must be submitted to the people on the demand of 30,000 citizens or eight cantons. The same applies to international treaties of 15 years or more in duration. In recent years, referendums were held on the average about 3 times a year.

With all this public involvement, the system proves to be remarkably conservative and stable. In fact, the Swiss voters are much more receptive to changes in the Constitution originating from the legislature than from public proposals. For example, between 1935 and 1960, eighteen out of twenty-six proposed changes by the legislature were accepted, while of popular proposals, only one out of twenty was accepted. Although the Swiss voters are very conservative about accepting proposals from public initiatives, they adamantly maintain their right to have such initiatives. As to stability, experience proved that many proposals must be submitted to Referendum several times before approval. Also, most proposals by public initiative are usually serious and large majorities usually reject extremist proposals.

It is remarkable that with this system, Switzerland has experienced the longest period of internal and external peace in Europe. This is even more remarkable since Switzerland is composed of three nationalities, French, German and Italian, countries that were often bitterly hostile to each other. Although cantons do have their official state religions, the Swiss majority never used its powers to repress ethnic or religious minorities. On the contrary, it provided a haven to European minorities who were the victims of Nazi persecution. The Swiss continue to experience ethnic peace while many parts of Europe and other countries are undergoing large-scale ethnic violence. Switzerland has also consistently maintained one of the highest standards of living in the world. Evidently, where all have equal say, people do not feel disenfranchised and threatened by fellow countrymen of other ethnic backgrounds.

Referendums and Initiatives are also the part of other western democracies in Europe. In the United States, 24 states and 100 cities have had initiatives and referendums. In some cases referendums and initiatives were used by weak governments that needed direct backing by the public for major decisions. In recent years, this occurred in such weakly democratic systems as Russia, Egypt and South Africa (white voters only). It is a curious irony that the governments of the most stable and historically entrenched democracies, such as the United States, Great Britain, Australia and New Zealand seem to be amongst the most resistant to use nationwide referendums, or to introduce nationwide Initiative powers.

The history of hundreds of Initiatives and referendums demonstrates that the voting public is fair, responsible and prudent. Some well-known examples are an Australian Constitutional Referendum that gave the Aboriginal minority the right to vote, with 78% of the voters casting their vote in favor of the referendum. In California, Proposition 13 in 1978 reduced property taxes substantially, but subsequent propositions for further tax reductions were rejected because the public understood the need to fund state services. In Italy, a referendum rejected automatic pay raises because the public understood the economic disadvantages.

Indeed, initiatives and referendums, even when not binding, tend to give direction to government policy. For example, the issue that was exposed to the broadest public voting in the United States was the Nuclear Freeze Initiatives. Although the outcome was not binding on government policy, the success of these referendums contributed to the atmosphere that brought about significant United States - USSR nuclear weapon reductions. Similarly, voters exerted pressure on environmental protection and other issues that were later reflected in policy on the national and state levels.

In summary, the overwhelming experience with public initiatives and referendums is that people take their responsibilities seriously, and make at least as prudent, stable and thoughtful decisions as elected governments.

Some important historical referendums

Some of the following notes were taken from the book The Referendum, by Jo Grimond and Brian Neve, 1975.

1788   United States In the state of Massachusetts the people were given the right to vote on new state constitutions or constitutional amendments. The other states followed suit.

1874   Switzerland Referendums and initiatives were adopted in the Swiss Constitution.

1898   United States South Dakota was the first state to adopt initiatives and referendums for ordinary legislation, with 19 other states following by 1928.

1901   Australia The Australian Constitution provided for the use of referendums only in changing the Constitution. This power has been used very conservatively. In 86 attempts to initiate constitutional amendments in the period 1901-1974, 54 of these lapsed or were defeated without being submitted to the voters. Of the remaining 32 attempts which were submitted to referendums, only five were accepted and eventually incorporated in the Constitution.

1916   Denmark Referendum approved the government's decision to transfer the Danish West Indies to the USA.

1905   Norway Two referendums were held in this year, one concerned the dissolution of the union with Sweden and the second on whether to institute a monarchical or republican regime.

1919   Norway A referendum resulted in the prohibition of alcohol. In 1926, another referendum repealed the prohibition law.

1922   Sweden The referendum procedure was introduced by a constitutional amendment.

1922   Sweden A narrow majority of voters voted against the introduction of prohibition of intoxicating liquors.

1937   Republic of Ireland Under the 1937 Constitution, a bill amending the Constitution must be submitted to an advisory referendum after passing both houses of Parliament.

1946   Italy   Post World War II groups favoring the monarchy insisted that the decision - between monarchic and republican forms of government - should be made by a national referendum. The referendum, on 2 June 1946, rejected the monarchy by a vote of 12,717,923 to 10,710,284.

1948   Italy The Constitution provided for referendums on constitutional laws or amendments to the Constitution.

1950   Belgium A referendum was held on the return of King Leopold III to the throne of Belgium, 58% of the population voted in his favor. He abdicated in favor of his son in 1951.

1953   Denmark Referendums became part of the constitution when, on giving up the upper house, Conservatives insisted on a provision for referendums as a check on the lower chamber.

1953   Denmark A national referendum changed the voting age to 23.

1955   Sweden In a 53% poll, an overwhelming majority rejected the idea that right hand driving should be substituted for left hand driving.

1957   Sweden A referendum was held on three competing schemes for a national pension scheme to re-enforce the basic benefits of old age pensions.

1958   France A new constitution (of the Fifth Republic) was drawn
        up and submitted to the people of France at a referendum.
        Under the new constitution, approved by 78% of the voters, the
        Presidency was strengthened and parliament weakened.

1961   France A Referendum was launched by President Charles de
        Gaulle to justify his decision to establish a provisional
        executive in Algeria.

1961   Denmark A referendum changed the voting age to 21.

1962   France A Referendum on an amendment to provide for direct
        election of the President, received 61.8% of the vote.

1967   New Zealand There was a referendum on a proposal to extend
        the parliamentary term from the existing 3-year maximum term
        to a 4-year term. No change was made.

1969   Denmark Referendum to reduce the voting age to 18 was
        substantially rejected. In 1971 the voting age was reduced to 20
        following a referendum.

1970   Italy Referendum was used to repeal existing laws. Article 75
        of the Constitution allows that if 500,000 electors demand a
        referendum it must be held. The opponents of the 1970
        Divorce Law had collected the 500,000 signatures required for
        the holding of a referendum to repeal the law.

1972   France Referendum to seek the views of the people on the
        enlargement of the European Community.

1972   Republic of Ireland Voted in favor of membership of the EEC.

1972   Norway A referendum was held to determine whether or not
        the country should join in full membership of the EEC. 53.5%
        of the electorate voted against Norway's full membership of the
        EEC and 46.5% voted in favor.

1974   Italy A referendum vote held to repeal the divorce law. The
        repeal was rejected.

1973   Australia A proposed constitutional amendment to give the
        Federal Government powers to control prices and incomes was
        defeated.

1992   New Zealand A referendum was held to decide on the electoral
        system from a range of electoral system options. The voters
        selected Mixed Member Proportional system (MMP) and
        rejected the First-Past-the-Post system.

Chapter 19

Ethical Foundations of Direct Democracy: Life-Centered Ethics and the Future

19.1 Life-Centered Ethics

Biotechnology can design new human traits. Such questions as "What is the human purpose?" and "What is essentially human and should be preserved?" will no longer be philosophical, but practical questions. For what should we aim when we re-design life? Should human nature and physiology be changed? What can be changed and what must be saved? Who should govern these powers?

The answer to these questions should start with a definition of the human purpose based on the common denominator that unites all humans: *we all belong to Life.* This most basic human identity leads to a Life-centered ethics.

Life is a process whose essence is self-propagation. The central biochemical process is the genetic coding of proteins which in return help to replicate the genetic code. The act of self-replication is equivalent to the pursuit of a purpose. These mechanisms are shared by all cellular beings. Although the biomolecules have no foresight, by all observable means the outcome is equivalent to action with a purpose. This insight is the scientific basis that identifies the purpose and unity of all Life.

Life has a unique value in Nature. Biological structures and processes are unique in their complexity. Living matter is miniscule in quantity, but qualitatively it is the summit of Nature. The biological process depends on many features of the physical universe that are finely tuned in a way that just allows Life to exist. Whether this is a spectacular coincidence or the act of a purposeful Creator, Life is uniquely precious. Based on these principles we can define a panbiotic human purpose that seeks to maximize life in the universe.

Those acts that promote Life are good; those that endanger and destroy Life are evil.
It is the human purpose to forever safeguard Life, and to propagate Life throughout the universe.

The Principles of Life-Centered Ethics

1. Life is a process of active self-propagation by organic molecular patterns.
2. The patterns of organic Life are embodied in biomolecules that actively reproduce through cycles of genetic information and protein action.
3. But action that leads to a selected outcome is equivalent to the pursuit of a purpose. Where there is Life there is therefore purpose.
4. The purpose of Life is self-propagation; the purpose of Life is to live.
5. Humans are part of the family of organic Life, all of whom share the cellular mechanisms of life and procreation.
6. The human purpose must be self-defined by human beings.
7. The human purpose is best defined by the purpose of all Life, self-propagation.
8. Therefore the human purpose is to forever safeguard and propagate Life and to establish the living pattern as a governing force throughout the universe.
9. The human purpose defines the principles of ethics. Moral good is that which promotes Life, and evil is that which destroys Life.
10. Life, in the complexity of its structures and processes, is unique amongst the hierarchy of structures in Nature. This unites the family of Life and raises it above the inanimate universe.
11. Life is made possible only by a precise coincidence of the laws of physics. Thereby the physical universe comes to a special point in the living process.
12. Life-forms who are most fit, survive and reproduce best. Selection by survival is the logic of Life.
13. Whether controlled by random mutation or by human design, living beings will be always judged by the logic of survival.
14. Whereas the mechanisms of Life may change, the logic of Life is permanent.
15. Survival is best secured by expansion in space, and biological progress is best assured by diversification in new worlds, environments and habitats.
16. Adaptation to space will necessitate human/machine coexistence. However, control must always remain vested in organic intelligences with self-interest to continue the organic life-form.

17. When conscious human decisions will rule the future, Life can persist only if the will to propagate is itself always propagated.
18. The future is best assured by the instincts of survival inherited from the lessons of evolution and deeply imprinted in human nature. This legacy is best reflected in the wisdom distilled from the common human will.
19. The human purpose and the destiny of Life are intertwined. The results can light up the galaxy with life, and affect the future patterns of the universe.
20. When, through human action, Life pervades all Nature, human existence will have attained a cosmic purpose.

19.2 Biotechnology and Survival

The value of Life is intrinsic in our instincts, it has been central to ethics and religion since antiquity and is now amplified by science. The purpose to propagate Life may therefore be accepted universally.

Having defined this basic human purpose allows us to judge biotechnology. Does genetic engineering facilitate or endanger the survival of humankind and of Life? It does both, most profoundly.

Continuation depends on our drive for procreation. This is the source of parental love; of the desire for self-continuation and immortality, if not of our bodies, at least of our genes; of the pursuit of healthy sexual pleasures. If human nature is altered, these instincts may be lost. Instead, mis-engineered post-humans may find pleasure in drugs, virtual reality, electric simulation of the brain, and self-serving intellectual pursuits.

The success of our species derives from a unique combination of empathy, aggression and intelligence. Without empathy, society cannot function; without aggression, we cannot progress and expand; and intelligence creates the required technology to achieve those ends. If these traits are mis-engineered, our species may decay into lethargy or self-destruct in excessive aggression.

On the other hand, genetic engineering may cure all disease and grant us permanent youth. Beyond this, it will be the key to living in outer space, which is the ultimate guarantor of survival as Life expands into many independent habitats. True adaptation to space will require new physiologies. The needed traits will include survival in high vacuum, extreme temperatures and tolerance for increased radiation; direct biological use of solar energy similar to the ways in which plants on earth utilize sunlight for photosynthesis, and a closed internal recycling of all wastes; locomotion by solar sailing. Other traits will be needed in planetary environments. Indeed, as noted above, "Homo Sapiens" will give rise to new species, which could be called "Homo Spaciens" (or, being born of space and science, "Homo Spascience").

These extensive physiological changes can be achieved only through genetic engineering. It is much faster than natural mutations, and also allows evolution without pain. Natural selection involves suffering by those who carry bad mutations. This can be avoided by designed evolution.

Note however, that natural selection will always prevail. It is based on the tautology that the survivors prevail, the failures perish. Whether natural or designed evolution, this logic will ultimately choose which of our successor species will continue. Indeed, survival will ultimately judge if engineered evolution is a success or failure.

19.3   Genetic Engineering and Direct Democracy

The pursuit of our future is consistent with both scientific and religious views. The Old Testament states that: "Be fruitful and multiply and replenish the Earth" (Genesis 2, 28), and: "I have set before you life and death, blessing and curse: therefore choose life, that both you and your seed may live" (Deuteronomy 30, 19). The sanctity and unity of Life is also central to Buddhism. On the side of secular humanism, Julian Huxley in "Religion without Revelation" defines the human purpose as "the realization of more evolutionary possibilities by more and more fully developed individuals."

To secure our success, we must make sure that genetic engineering is governed safely. What form of government can direct this power most prudently? The most fair and safe system is public debate and communal decision, for the following reasons.

Through natural selection, human behavior became focussed on the needs of living. Those who value these needs most are the ones most likely to propagate best. Through the logic of selection, human nature came to respect Life, abhor death, and value comfort, food and shelter. Above all, we value and protect the young who will continue our propagation. The common will reflects these basic values.

Indeed, the record of public decisions is moderate and prudent. As a recent example, the Swiss public voted in referendum on May 17, 1992, by a margin of 74%, for "an article that prohibits gene technology manipulation which may in any way endanger the nobility of Creation and the safety of humankind, animals and the environment. Especially, there shall be no intervention with human reproductive cells and embryonic life...(Such work) is permitted only by specific legislation and with the permission of the individual involved".

In another test of public attitudes, a group of adult students were surveyed on related questions, as reported in The Futurist, July-August 1992, p.41 - 44. The questionnaire described such utopias as indefinite life span, genius-level intelligence for all, work done by robots and permanent holidays and no work for people, and populations moving to prosperous space colonies. These apparently desirable changes were rejected by most of the respondents. The more these developments deviated from the natural human condition, the stronger was the objection. The utopias were rejected because they were dehumanizing. In the end, the results reflected the main human driving force to protect and perpetuate our species.

The survey was done in New Zealand and duplicated in Western Washington University with similar results. The responses reflected human instincts so deep that similar results would probably be obtained by public polls an any scale, extending even to a global public opinion poll.

In contrast to the prudent decisions by public referendums and polls, dictators and zealots may abuse genetic engineering in various ways. Dictators may rush into biotechnology to duplicate themselves, and the world may face millions of copies of the likes of Hitler and Stalin. Capitalist extremists may create billions of recklessly greedy consumers and mindless slaves to exploit as cheap labor. Ideological zealots of all kinds may seek to create masses of feeble, unquestioning followers. The best safeguard against such abuses is the open and public control of biotechnology.

19.4 Principles of Biodemocracy

The above arguments justify why biodemocracy, the democratic management of biotechnology, is vital. How can such direct democracies be instituted?

First, the various features of Direct Democracy, i.e., referendums and polls, should be brought to public debate much more intensively than it is at present. That the public is interested in these issues is evidenced by popular science fiction, but the futuristic tone of the subject has not inspired serious public discussion so far.

Can the public understand and judge scientific issues? The Public Agenda Foundation in New York researched this subject on issues such as waste disposal, education, criminal justice and transportation. They found that after a few hours of education, public panels arrived at the same opinions as panels of technically educated individuals. This shows that the public is capable of judging complex issues. It is also important to realize that human genetic intervention is primarily a moral issue. One does not need to understand the technical details to judge the consequences.

Some practical measures of public debate could be implemented at this time. Gene therapy and especially inheritable germ-line intervention should be discussed frequently in the media and on television and radio talk shows. A branch of the US National Institute of Health (NIH) should be dedicated to public education and to surveying public opinion.

The ethical significance of the issue is well recognized. For example, the Human Genome Project reserves 3% of its budget to research the ethical implications by bioethics "experts". The same support, or more, should be dedicated to public education. Public opinion should be solicited, researched and the results considered in deciding genetic research policy. Ultimately, it should be *mandatory* that experiments and/or processes of human genetic intervention be subject to balanced public debate and national referendums. This will require instituting national initiatives and referendums in the United States and in other nations where this is still lacking.

Indeed, the consequences of genetic intervention will go beyond national boundaries. Once an artificial gene or a gene from another species is introduced into the population anywhere, it is bound to spread globally. The shared human genetic future is at stake and as such, it should be subject to global referendums.

19.5 Biodemocracy and Our Genetic Future

Human genetic engineering, more than any other technology, will affect the future of our species and of Life itself. This technology will be motivated by the fight against disease, hunger and aging, and ultimately by adaptation to the space environment. While biotechnology may be the ultimate guarantor of survival, it also presents the ultimate danger of mis-engineering humans who may lose the drive to propagate, or who may self-destruct through excessive aggression. Other technologies that may endanger human survival, such as takeover by intelligent and hardy robots must be also controlled.

The success of genetic engineering will be judged by the logic of natural selection and survival. If this next phase in the history of Life is to be a success, an ethical code must be instituted that will consciously seek the propagation of Life as the ultimate human purpose.

Until such ethics are firmly established, the fateful new technologies must be controlled by the shared human drive to preserve and propagate the species. Only this common sense can guarantee that these powerful technologies are not developed beyond control in secret and are not taken over by fanatics or zealots. To serve humanity and Life, these forces are best secured through public debate and decision making, which distils the basic drives of Life that are common to all human beings.

Our genetic future is collective. The combination of genes that defines any individual diffuses in the population with time; what survives is the shared collective pool of human genes. Everyone should have an equal say in deciding the future of this shared human genetic heritage, and through it, the future of Life to which we all belong.

19.6 Life-Centered Ethics, the Human Purpose, and Our Future

In the coming centuries, humanity faces profound decisions: democracy or totalitarianism; mass weapons or disarmament; religious freedom or fundamentalism; genetic modification, robots, space colonies, population growth and even immortality.

Our decisions will control the future of humanity, even the future of Life. These decisions will be formulated by human society, by its laws and government. These institutions must be able to serve our survival and progress. This is best assured by a system that reflects the common wisdom that is rooted in the human drives for security, physical sustenance, dignity, survival and procreation. Communal decisions distil this shared human wisdom from the diverse wishes of people. By this argument, Direct Democracy derives from the most basic interests of humanity and of all Life.

To decide the course of the future, basic questions must be answered. What is the essence of being human? What can be changed and what must be preserved to keep us human? What is the human purpose?

The most basic fact about humans is that we all belong to the family of living beings. Therefore, the human purpose must be consistent with the purpose of Life itself.

Does Life have a purpose? In fact, Life is characterized by a purpose. Life pursues self-perpetuation, and the acts of life are equivalent to pursuing this purpose. Intrinsic to Life therefore there is a purpose, self-propagation.

From our identity as living beings we can derive the principles of ethics and of the human purpose. Good is that which promotes Life, and evil is that which threatens and destroys Life. The human purpose is to forever safeguard and propagate Life, and to elevate Life into a controlling force in the universe.

The principles of such a panbotic ethics are consistent with the appreciation of life and the abhorrence of death and murder shared by all major religions and civilizations. Because of the appreciation of Life, a Life-centered ethics can be accepted by most of humanity. Our shared appreciation of life assures that communal decisions will serve Life.

The instinctive appreciation of Life arose from natural selection: those who pursue survival and propagation pass on their genes to the next generations. Those who derive pleasure from survival and propagation pursue these ends most diligently. We find pleasure and happiness in food, physical comfort, in procreation and in raising the next generation. The logic of the living process linked pleasure to survival and propagation. These drives are the foundations of human nature.

While there are many cultures, we all share our common needs: food, shelter, health and security. When making decisions on issues, these basic needs are distilled from the diverse motivations of people. The communal decisions reflect the needs of survival and serve Life.

The need for social status also emerges from competition and natural selection. These needs are expressed as honor and dignity. Most people prefer to live in a society that respects human dignity, since this assures that their own dignity will be respected.

The right of self-determination is essential to dignity. This right must be limited to maintain social order. To maintain maximum dignity, no individual should impose these laws over others. The most dignified way to formulate laws is by communal decisions in which everyone has an equal share.

When human needs and dignity are satisfied by shared decisions, people are content. Therefore communal decisions minimize conflict and protect peace. In our times, with mass weapons, peace is essential for our survival, and with it, the survival of all life. In this manner, communal decisions serve the highest moral good, the perpetuation of life.

Ultimately, our ethics will be decided by a shared vision of humanity. As the values of Life are central to human nature, we can expect that this will be consistent with Life-centered ethics.

Communal decisions are based on the instincts of survival, and on our shared appreciation of life, peace and human dignity. When charged with the future of Life the basic human desires, expressed through communal decisions, will guide us best to serve Life. Communal decisions will also best assure justice, peace and human dignity.

These principles connect life-centered ethics and Direct Democracy. They may be summarized by three simple tenets.

Love Life
Respect Reality
Honor Human Dignity

Chapter 20
Direct Democracy and The Human Future

A ll people contribute to the human future. The course of that future, and indeed of the history of Life itself, is now at a turning point. From this time on, it will be human decisions that will shape human evolution and the future development of Life, on Earth and throughout the universe. These decisions will shape the future of our descendants, carrying forth the shared human genetic heritage. This future is the ultimate outcome of all of our lives' efforts, and all should have an equal say in shaping this shared future.

Human life, and human nature itself, may be changed. Our intelligence may be increased through genetic manipulation and by computers implanted in brains; robots designed to do our work may attempt to take control; we may acquire extended senses to enhance our aesthetic experience.

Ultimately, we may eliminate all disease and aging. This will further increase the population and motivate the move to space. From enclosed Earth-like habitats, future humans will emerge through genetic engineering as truly space-adapted life forms. Homo Sapiens will transform itself into Homo Spacience, (or, being adapted to space through science, into "Homo Spascience"). In a variety of new worlds, our descendants will branch into divergent species, all co-existing in peace afforded by limitless resources. The seeds of organic Life will be sent to new Solar Systems in the Galaxy. Ultimately, Life will permeate through the universe and control the future of the cosmos.

From the perspective of human values, the magnitude of future change will be incomprehensible. For example, aging is a biochemical process that can be unraveled and altered. Assume that an individual can live for a thousand years in perfect youthful vigor. If death is rare and people don't have to be replaced, how many children will then be needed and who may have them? How long will a couple live together? How many years will an individual work? How will people stave off boredom? What will young people feel towards a great-great-great-grandparent who is just as young as they are?

Clearly, the human future springs from all of us. Human decisions will control the future of Life itself. It is vital to establish who will formulate the decisions that will control this future.

Despite the broad implications of biotechnology there is very limited discussion, mostly confined to scientists and "experts" on bioethics and about human genetic engineering. This, despite the fact that bioethics attracts much public interest as attested by the media coverage of topics such as "test-tube babies", artificial insemination, surrogate mothers, euthanasia; Dolly, the cloned sheep and related science fiction topics on brain transplant and life extension.

Nevertheless, science is moving with increasing momentum, immune from public scrutiny. It promises extended life spans, increased intelligence and robots that will perform all labor. Scientists and funding governments presume that these alterations of the human experience are universally desired. Since the experts presume to know what people want, there is little effort to actually ask the public for their opinions.

The author had an occasion to put this issue to a test, in a limited manner. The test was given in the context of a series of lectures on "Think Biggest: Grand Designs for the Future", given at the Continuing Education Department of the University of Canterbury in Christchurch, New Zealand. The audience was evidently not a random sample, and was in fact as you would predict the participants in a future-oriented class was likely be, i.e., as open-minded as any group. The audience ranged in age from the 20's to the 70's, mostly with a secondary education and technical training but not academic professions (typically the group consisted of teachers, nurses, technicians, secretaries, unemployed and retired people). 25 - 35 respondents answered each question.

The class dealt with these main topics: the large-scale settlement of space, the nature of Life as a complex biochemical process and the value of Life as a unique phenomenon in the Universe. Genetic engineering and its consequences, which are included the questionnaire (except space colonization) were not covered in the course. There were no prior discussions on these issues that would have influenced the respondents' opinions.

The following is a list of the questions from the questionnaire. The respondents were asked to rank each future trend from "very desirable" to "very undesirable". The responses were divided into:

- favorable   (weighted **+1**),
- neutral   (weighted **0**) and
- unfavorable   (weighted **-1**).

The sum of answers was normalized to the number of respondents in a manner that the ratings can range from +100% (very desirable) to -100% (very unfavorable). In addition, the respondents were also asked to make verbal comments on the questions.

The questions, respondent ratings and typical comments are summarized as follows:

Questionnaire on the Human Future

Instructions:
The following developments may happen during the next 100 years. Rank from very desirable to very undesirable

A. Genetic Engineering	Rating
1. Genetic engineering is applied to improve plants and livestock.	+87
2. Non-inheritable genes are implanted in patients to cure dwarfism.	+30
3. Non-inheritable genes are implanted in patients to prevent heart disease.	+22
4. Inheritable (germ-line) genes are implanted in susceptible families against dwarfism.	+32
5. Inheritable genes are implanted in susceptible families to prevent heart disease.	+26
6. Inheritable genes are implanted in the whole population to prevent all diseases.	+8
7. Genetic engineering cures all disease and hunger.	+30

8. Genetic engineering eliminates all disease and hunger and changes humans into a different species.   -34

9. New super-humans are developed with superior intelligence and physical fitness.   -21

10 Genetic engineering of one's family is allowed by individual decision.   -14

11. No interference with human genetics is allowed for any reason.   0

12. The genetic development of all living things is left up to Nature.   -14

B. Intelligence	Rating

1. The IQs of retarded patients are raised to normal levels.   +13

2. The IQs of the whole population is raised by 10 points.   0

3. The IQs of the whole population are raised by 100 points (to genius level).   -44

4. Any individual is permitted to have his/her IQ raised as desired.   -18

5. Human intelligence is increased by computers implanted in the brain.   -71

C. Life Expectancy	Rating

1. Life expectancy increases to 200 years.   -6

2. Life expectancy becomes indefinite.   -61

D. Population and Reproduction	**Rating**
1. Population is allowed to grow freely and stabilize naturally by disease, war, and famine.	-59
2. One child per family is enforced by compulsory sterilization.	-61
3. Natural reproduction is replaced by test-tube babies.	-73

E. Robots	**Rating**
1. Robots do all menial jobs, 2-day workweek for people.	-6
2. Robots do all work, people on permanent vacation.	-66
3. Robots are developed who are superior to people, but are controlled by people.	-47
4. Ordinary humans, super-humans and robots share the world.	-10
5. Ordinary humans, super-humans and robots co-exist on separate worlds.	-36
6. Robots with superior strength and intelligence replace living beings, and proceed to populate the universe.	-77

F. Life in Space	**Rating**
1. Most people live in space colonies with advanced living standards.	-3
2. Humankind populates the universe.	0
3. Advanced post-humans replace humankind and proceed to populate the universe.	-25

G. Controlling the Future	Rating

1. Government by intelligent super-computer.   -79

2. Prohibiting or permitting and regulating human genetic engineering should be decided by:
    a. The government.   -100

    b. Panels of experts (doctors, scientists, judges, the clergy, etc.).   0

    c. General public panels.   -62

    d. Public referendums.   -38

    e. International global convention and treaty.   -20

3. The future should be allowed to take its own course (without controls).   -25

4. Laws should be enacted by society to control the future.   -18

The results reflect a general trend. The more extreme the changes are from the present human condition, the more negative were the responses. Even in this open-minded audience, a deep vein of conservatism ran against any basic changes to human features. Surprisingly, this applies even to developments that cater to common aspirations.

For example, the fear of death is the most common instinct, yet the offer of an indefinite life span was rated -61. While everyone would like to be smarter, making superior intelligence available for all was rated -44. Even though many people disdain menial work and dream of vacations and retirement, the question about having robots liberating people from all work was rated -66. People seem to perceive such "improvements" as dehumanizing. What would emerge may be improved, but it would not be human. These options were rejected, probably by the instinct to preserve the species.

Comments made by many of the respondents stressed the need to improve human values rather than to make technological advances, or they felt ready to accept the advances only if they promoted human values. For example, intelligence levels should be raised only if this improves socio-human values; robots and computers should not rule because they lack emotions; life-span should increase only if the quality of life increases; "superhumans" should be enlightened, humane and loving. Given the state of the environment, on "humankind populates the universe", a respondent commented "God help the universe." Similar to the gradings, the verbal comments expressed strong reservations about extreme changes.

Robots will help people but may also threaten us. Machines may be partially fused with humans. How far can we go? In our survey, "robots replace humans" received a rating of -77. The more technology changes the human condition, the less people approve. With Direct Democracy, our common concern for the future will direct technology to serve but not to threaten human survival.

Although the sample of respondents was limited, the answers appear to reflect deeply seated human feelings. Indeed, the survey was repeated in a class in Western Washington University with similar results. It is therefore quite possible that a public referendum, probably in any nation or done globally, would have a similar outcome.

Nevertheless, science keeps advancing in these directions. Scientists are driven by curiosity, ambition and a sense of power. Scientists also desire to serve humankind - in a manner that they define or at least assume to represent progress. Consulting the public is not desirable, possibly for the fear of restrictions on research, and to many scientists the freedom of inquiry is sacred.

Yet science is a human enterprise, and like all other human enterprises, it should serve Life first. If the communal sense of survival feels threatened, then the dangers should be considered seriously. In any event the communal will, should at least be consulted as a first step. If a conflict should arise between the survival of Life and the freedom of the spirit, then the former must prevail; since without Life there exists no spirit that could enjoy freedom.

Evidently, the future of Life is the most basic issue of all and in which every living human being has a vested interest. This is the basic argument for biodemocracy - *The democratic management of human biotechnology*.

The future is in space, and new worlds will require genetic adaptation. Our decisions will control the evolution of our species, and maybe the future of all Life itself in the universe. The basic respect for Life, as reflected in the communal human will, can best guide our ultimate destiny.

The Constitution (Continued)

Part VII
The Constitution (Continued)

The first four parts of the model Constitution were presented at the beginning of this book.

Section 5   Procedures

Article I   Public Decision Making

Section I.1   Defining the Issues

1. The public itself must define the agenda for public voting.

2. Each voter may submit three proposal issues a year for public voting and preferred policies on these issues to the National Proposal Bank. The voter may submit an original request or support one already on the List of Proposals.

3. The National Proposal Bank will sort, classify and tally the proposals according to subject or theme. A proposal may be found to pertain to several subjects/themes in which case the proposing citizen will be notified of the classification and if they disagree with the classification they will be able to change it.

4. The five most requested issues from the public will be subject to national referendums. The next twenty issues will be subject to a poll.

5. Five referendum issues and twenty poll issues may be requested by the Executive Council.

6. If 100,000 voters request a proposal issue within any two-month period it will immediately be subject to an Emergency Referendum. It the issue is requested by 50,000 voters, it will be subject to an Emergency Poll.

7. A Budget Referendum will decide the major divisions of the National Budget. The public will assign relative priorities by voting on a "pie chart" (percentage) basis. Changes from the preceding Budget may be limited. Taxation will be part of the Budget Referendum.

Section I.2   Public Debates

1. Public decision-making must be informed and well reasoned. To this effect there will be public debates preceding the referendums.

2. Debates will be held during the two-month Debate Period immediately preceding the referendum. The Debates Agency will coordinate the debates.

3. The Debates Agency will appoint an Issue Panel for each referendum and poll issue. The members of each panel will include qualified advocates for each of the major policy options and representatives from the general public.

4. The Issue Panel will define policy options extracted from the public proposals or corresponding to issues raised by the Expert Agencies, narrow the list of issue options to three, formulate the wording of the referendum or poll questions and prepare the public debate materials.

5. If the Issue Panel fails to narrow the list of options on any issue to three, a pre-referendum Screening Poll will be held to choose the three most popular options.

6. The Debates Agency will select by random lot, members to a Referendum Jury or Poll Jury for each referendum and poll issue. The number of members should statistically represent a cross-section of the public. The role of the jury and the Public Ombudsman is to certify that all the material prepared by the Issue Panel is informative, factual, balanced and non-manipulative.

7. The Debates Agency will assure that the debate material is disseminated to all voters and prominently publicized. Incentives may be used to encourage voter attendance. The debate materials must reach all voters, unless the citizen expressly wishes to be excluded.

Section I.3   Referendums and Polls

1. The Referendum and Poll Agency will manage the conduct of referendums and polls. The Referendum and Poll Agency will assure the orderly conduct of referendums and polls and the accurate tallying of the votes.

2. Voters will vote by rating each policy alternative. The highest rated alternative will become the law.

3. Voters may label any or all the policy alternatives as "unacceptable". If all policy alternatives are so labeled by the majority of voters, the referendum will be void.

4. Referendums will be conducted during a 30-day period following the two-month debate period. Citizens may vote on any referendums, together or separately, at any time during the referendum-voting period.

5. The Referendum and Poll Agency will assure that all citizens can vote without hindrance and with the greatest possible convenience. Tele-voting and computer network voting from the home will be encouraged.

6. Towards the end of the 30-day referendum voting period, the Referendum and Poll Agency will contact all citizens who have not voted and solicit their votes. However, participation will not be forced. Citizens can request not to be contacted by the Referendum and Poll Agency.

7. Polls will be conducted using Poll Respondents, a random group of voters that is large enough to be statistically representative of the public.

8. Poll Respondents will receive debate materials prepared by the Issue Panels. The respondents will receive the material at least fourteen days before the Poll is conducted. Additional debate materials and information are available for Poll Respondents from the Expert Agencies, if needed.

9. The identities of Poll Respondents may remain anonymous upon request, except for disclosure to the Public Ombudsman for verification. Poll Respondents will vote anonymously.

Article II   Expert Management

Section II.1   Policy Juries

1. Expert Agencies will execute the laws and policies enacted by the voters.

2. Adjunct to each Expert Agency will be a Policy Jury. Jurors will be selected randomly. The number of Jurors in the Policy Jury will be large enough to be a representative statistical cross-section of the voting public.

3. The Policy Jury will advise the Expert Agency on major decisions, intervene in actions of the Expert Agency that are found to be inconsistent with the public will, and adjudicate disputes between the Public Ombudsman and the Expert Agency.

4. Policy Jurors will receive education in the Expert Agency's area of expertise. The majority of the Jurors at any time will be experienced, as each Policy Juror will serve for a term of four years with one-quarter of the Jury being replaced each year.

5. The Jury will meet by teleconferencing. Jurors will at most, work three evenings per week and will be compensated.

6. The Policy Jury will:
    - Allocate the major divisions of the Expert Agency's budget;
    - Review any project that involves over 2 percent of the budget of the Expert Agency and

- Review any action of the Expert Agency that affects more than one percent of the population.

7. The Policy Jury will vote whether to hear matters requested by more than five but less then ten percent of the Jurors. The Policy Jury will hear any matter requested by ten percent or more of the Jurors.

8. The number of interventions the Jury can take in the actions of the Agency will be limited.

9. The Policy Jury will hear, or vote not to hear, appeals of disputes between the Expert Agencies and the Courts.

10. Decisions of the Policy Jury will be made by majority vote, with a quorum of sixty percent.

11. The Head of an Expert Agency may veto any decision reached by less than sixty percent of the voting Jurors. This veto may itself be overturned by a seventy-five percent quorum of Jurors.

Section II.2   Expert Agencies

1. The Budget and Taxation Agency will formulate specific tax laws and allocate the Budget among the various Expert Agencies and to specific programs in accordance with the public guidelines of the Budget Referendum.

2. The International Affairs Expert Agency will manage treaties, diplomatic transactions and consular affairs.

3. The Defense and Survival Expert Agency will maintain such forces and equipment as is necessary to protect the citizens from foreign threats and natural disasters.

4. The Domestic Peace Expert Agency will enforce the law and the decisions of the Expert Agencies and the Judiciary, and protect the citizens from crime and terrorism.

5. The Human Rights Expert Agency will assure that law and justice are applied equally to all.

6. The Human Services Expert Agency will secure that the basic necessities of food, shelter, clothing, and education are provided to all.

7. The Health Services Expert Agency will assure that health care is accessible to all, and provide for health research.

8. The Science and Technology Expert Agency will provide funding for research and development in the service of knowledge and survival, subject to guidelines and constraints enacted by the voting public.

9. The Environment Expert Agency will protect and manage the natural environment.

10. The Commerce, Trade and Labor Expert Agency will assure that economic activities are practiced equitably and fairly.

11. The Local Governments Expert Agency will manage the interaction of the Expert Agencies with local communities and governments.

12. The National Proposal Bank, the Debates Agency and the Referendum and Poll Agency will assure the orderly and efficient conduct of public decision-making and the election of public officials.

13. The General Management Expert Agency will manage all matters not covered by the other Agencies.

14. The public will elect a Head of each Expert Agency to one term of ten years. Candidates will need to possess at least ten years of experience in the area of expertise of the Agency, including five years of experience in management.

Section II.3   The Executive Council and Emergency Management

1. The Executive Council will allocate the jurisdictions of the Expert Agencies and arbitrate disputes amongst the Agencies.

2. The Executive Council will be comprised of the Heads of the Expert Agencies and an equal number of members-at-large each elected by the public to one ten-year term. There will also be an Executive Ombudsman, elected according to the guidelines set down in paragraph 6 of this Section.

3. The Executive Council will elect a coordinator from its members for a one-term year. The coordinator will be responsible for scheduling and chairing the meetings of the Executive Council.

4. The Executive Council will formulate up to five referendum issues and twenty poll issues and related policy options annually. These issues will arise from the Executive Council itself, from the Expert Agencies and the Public Ombudsman, or from disputes among these agencies.

5. Responses to foreseeable types of emergencies will be formulated in advance by the public through referendums.

6. An Executive Ombudsman will be elected for one ten-year term. Candidates will need to demonstrate fifteen years of high-level expertise in defense and civil defense management.

7. Major public emergencies will be managed by the Executive Ombudsman under the pre-established public guidelines until such time that the Executive Council can assume control, no later than two days after the onset of the emergency.

8. The Executive Council will manage the emergency until an Emergency Referendum can be conducted, no later than two weeks after the onset of the emergency.

9. Other than an emergency response to military attacks, war must be declared by at least seventy percent of the vote in each of two

consecutive referendums separated by seven days. This applies to entry to wars mandated by defense treaties.

Article III   The Judiciary

Section III.1   Expert Courts

1. Courts will be expert in their field of jurisdiction.

2. Expert Courts will adjudicate disputes among individuals and organizations.

3. Decisions of the specialist Expert Courts may be appealed to the Supreme Courts.

4. A Chief Justice who is elected by the public to one ten-year term will head each Expert High Court. Candidates must demonstrate ten years of experience in corresponding area of specialized jurisprudence.

5. Corresponding to each Expert Agency will be an Expert Court that will adjudicate disputes between citizens, or the Public Ombudsman, and the Agency.

6. Decisions of the Expert Courts can be appealed to their associated Policy Jury.

Section III.2   Supreme Court and Ethics Court

1. The Supreme Court is composed of emeritus Expert Justices and emeritus Chiefs of Expert Agencies and the Chief Justices of the Expert Courts.

2. When needed, these members are constituted into Expert Panels to deal with issues that require specialized knowledge.

3. Decisions of the Supreme Court can be appealed through proposals for referendums and polls to the ultimate authority, the voting public.

4. Life sentences, death sentences and Supreme Court and Policy Jury decisions with clear individual life-and-death consequences may be appealed to a public Ethics Jury. The Ethics Jury will be similar in composition and procedure to the Policy Juries.

5. Decisions of the Supreme Court, Policy Juries and the Ethics Jury may be appealed to the highest authority of the voting public, through petition to the Executive Council for a Referendum or Poll. Each such referendum or poll will count as one of the annual referendums or polls allowed to the Executive Council.

Article IV   Election and Removal of Officials

1. Officials shall be elected on merit, by qualifications and attitudes to relevant issues, regardless of the unrelated aspect of personality.

2. Candidates for elected office must posses at least ten years of relevant experience.

3. Candidates must register with the Elections Agency at least six months prior to the elections. The Elections Agency will investigate and certify that the qualifications of the candidates meet the set standards.

4. For each office, the Elections Agency will select eight candidates by lot from the list of qualified candidates. Pairs of candidates will be screened in Nomination Polls to select four semi-final and then two final candidates.

5. The two final candidates will stand for election by public vote during the National Referendum.

6. At all the stages of nominations and elections, the candidates will be anonymous. The Screening Poll Respondents and the electorate will be informed of the pertinent qualifications and record of the candidates.

7. The compensation of elected officials will be appropriate for managers based on a salary scale approved by referendum.

8. Elected officials can be removed by a 70 percent vote in a Removal Referendum. Such referendums can be initiated by public proposals, tallied as other proposals; or by the Public Ombudsman and the majority of the Executive Council.

9. Removal referendums will be debated and processed similar to general referendums.

10. Unscheduled vacancies will be filled by the Executive Council until elections are held.

Article V   Checks and Balances and Stability

1. Laws, even when passed by the majority of the public, may nevertheless be unreasonable. Therefore the Executive Council may veto public decisions, but the veto may be overturned by a large majority of the public.

2. Any referendum alternative that has been approved by less than sixty percent of the vote, or in a poll by less than seventy percent of the vote, can be overturned in favor of another alternative. The vote can be annulled through a veto by eighty percent of the Executive Council. The veto must occur within sixty days after the public decision.

3. The veto of a referendum decision will be subject to a referendum in the next referendum period, and may be overturned by seventy percent of popular the vote.

4. The veto of a poll decision will be subject to a repeat poll within three month after the veto, and may be overturned by an eighty-percent vote of the Poll Respondents.

5. Other than the veto procedure, a law passed by referendum can be changed only by another referendum. A law passed by a poll, may be changed by a referendum or a poll.

6. An issue subject to a Referendum may not be subject to another Referendum for four years. An issue subject to a Poll may not be subject to another Referendum or Poll for two years.

Article VI   Amendments to the Constitution

1. The Constitution shall be amended only upon sustained demand by a substantial majority vote.

2. A referendum to amend the Constitution must be requested by public proposals submitted by two percent of the voters for two consecutive years or by eighty percent of the Executive Council for four consecutive years.

3. Amendment Referendums will be debated during National Referendums. An amendment will be passed by seventy percent of the public vote in two Amendment Referendums separated by two years. The quorum for Amendment Referendums will be seventy percent of the eligible voters.

4. A Constitutional law will not be amended more than once every ten years.

5. This Constitution shall become valid after approval the by seventy percent of the vote in two consecutive Constitutional Referendums separated by two years. The quorum will be seventy percent of the eligible voters.

Letterhead of the first Direct Democracy Campaign 1984 in the Maryland District Six Congressional race.

HELENE D. MAUTNER FOR CONGRESS
Maryland District Six

P.O. Box 3263
Gaithersburg, Maryland 20878
(301) 963-8261

Direct Democracy:
– LET THE PEOPLE DECIDE –

"On every major issue, I shall poll my constituents and vote in Congress strictly as instructed by the majority."

Part VIII Appendix

Appendix 1
A Symbolic Direct Democracy Campaign

The First Direct Democracy Campaign

The Candidate's Pledge to the Public

"On every major issue, I shall poll my constituents and vote in Congress strictly as instructed by the majority."

1984 Campaign Pledge

Maryland, United States, District 6 Congressional District

The Story of the Campaign

In 1984 I registered as a candidate in the Democratic Primary for the District 6 Congressional seat in Maryland, U.S.A. as a Direct Democracy candidate. The decision to run in the primary under the Direct Democracy banner was based on several factors. We felt that the best way to publicize the ideas of DD and bring it directly to the people was through a political campaign. Political campaigns bring with it newspaper and radio coverage, invitations to speak to groups and legitimate reasons to stand in public places with the opportunity to "sell" the idea to passers-by.

Once the decision was made to launch a campaign, we next had to select a candidate to run on the Direct Democracy platform; someone who believed in its philosophy. My husband Michael, author of the present book, was anxious to put his name forward as a candidate until he found out that as a scientist working for the Government he was not allowed to run for public office. Being the only husband-and-wife "local chapter" it fell to me to pick up the baton and enter the race.

We chose to run in the Democratic Primary instead of the Republican Primary because there is a greater proportion of "liberal" or "open-minded" Democratic voters than Republicans, who as a group, tend to be more conservative. This was also the height of the arms race, and although most people believed (and prayed for) a reduction in nuclear weapons, the U.S. Government was headed by a Republican President who was convinced that nuclear war was "winnable", and actively promoted and financed such large-scale military programs as the "Star Wars" technology.

We believed that if our political system were truly democratic and the will of the people ruled, then politicians would be unable to make decisions which are contrary to the public will, and such dangerous policies as the nuclear arms race could not be enacted.

The objective of the campaign was to publicize the Direct Democracy philosophy and to introduce it to as many people as possible through meetings with community groups, small groups of neighbors and through direct contact with the voters. By officially registering and announcing the campaign, it brought the ideas to the attention of the press and radio providing the necessary publicity, which would otherwise be difficult to attain. It would have been nice to think that we had a chance to win, but up against the substantial campaign purses of organized political parties, we knew this was unlikely.

Although we did not solicit contributions (we ran the campaign at our own expense), a friend volunteered to act as the campaign treasurer. We did receive one donation for $15, which we promptly returned. We returned the donation in order to avoid the complex political campaign reporting requirements. Do not get the wrong idea; we are not against accepting contributions to Direct Democracy campaigns. In fact, the more money collected to promote and support these campaigns, the sooner we will see Direct Democracy representatives in office. There is no objection to collecting contributions when you know that the contributions cannot be used later on as a 'bribe" to the representative once in office. Contributing to a Direct Democracy campaign is like making a donation to an honorable charity, the return you get is to live in a more decent society.

There are two ways to get votes in a primary. One is by getting enough signatures on a petition, which allows your name to appear on the ballot. The other way is to run as a "write-in" candidate, where the voter writes your name in a place provided on the ballot. My aim was two-fold; I would try to get enough signatures to place my name on the ballot and at the same time, while collecting signatures, inform and introduce those voters I approached, to the ideas of Direct Democracy. With petition sheets in hand, I stood outside supermarkets, shops and other places frequented by the public and started to make my case for Direct Democracy.

My first surprise came with the ease at which people would speak to me about politics. Don't believe that people aren't interested in their government. Most people listened to my short description of how Direct Democracy would work, although not everyone signed the petition. Some who signed the petition told me that they didn't agree with what I had to say, but they felt I had a right to appear on the ballot. Acts of true democratic spirit!

Then there were the disillusioned voters, those people who were so let down by the behavior of politicians that they could not believe that politicians would actively consult their constituents and vote according to the majority will. When I told them that I would vote according to the majority will, they questioned how they could trust my promise when it is well known that most politicians will promise anything to get into office. This is in fact a common and not unfounded complaint. Such widespread beliefs about the general untrustworthiness of elected officials behoves Direct Democracy candidates to be people of honor and trust.

There were also those voters who were impressed with the ideas and principles of Direct Democracy but were pessimistic about whether politicians would give up their power so easily. I pointed out to them that the point of Direct Democracy was to elect those people who were not interested in power, but rather in the principles of true democracy. They readily agreed to this, but were still pessimistic about finding politicians who lacked the "lust for power". I told them that I was one such politician. Often, they then signed the petition.

As I hoped, my candidacy allowed me to speak to individuals and groups, some at more length. When I was able to spend a bit more time explaining the system, the most frequent doubt that they voiced was whether people would be well enough informed to make and advise on legislative issues. There was the general belief that Representatives with their advisers were better able to make those decisions. I did point out that frequently, in spite of the advice and information given to Representatives, their decisions on issues were based on the influence of pressure groups, lobbyists and PACs that contributed to their campaigns and kept them in office. There is also often pressure from other Representatives in a "you scratch my back I'll scratch yours" approach to legislative decision-making. I told them that the public would be fully informed about the issues through extensive debating and educational programs prior to a referendum vote.

The reactions I received from the random selection of people I spoke to were positive towards the idea of Direct Democracy, but doubtful about the reality of creating such a system. I think this doubt was due in part to the fact that the ideas and principles of Direct Democracy were new to them. Moreover, a short encounter on the street is insufficient time to go into detail about the system. I did hand out information sheets, but did not receive any feedback to this literature.

In the end I collected about five hundred signatures. About one in three people whom I spoke to signed the petition. My conclusions from this short study was that a political system based on Direct Democracy would be acceptable to most people, but too much is unknown by the public about how such a system would operate. *Running as a "Direct Democracy Representative" is in fact an efficient way to publicize the idea.* I did achieve some media coverage as shown in the article below. It is easy and worthwhile, even for individuals as myself. If there will be more such campaigns nationwide or worldwide, the media will pick it up and the exposure will help to further popularize the idea. My experience suggests that with support by Direct Democracy groups and with larger well-organized campaigns there may be a real chance to win seats in Congress or Parliaments. As the idea becomes more recognized and accepted, the public will be . introduced to Representatives who truly "ask their constituents for their opinions" and, more importantly "vote in Congress or Parliament according to the majority view of their constituents". When people see Direct Democracy Representatives in action, the public will believe that the system can really work.

Appendix 2
Campaign Materials for Direct Democracy Candidates

HELENE D. MAUTNER FOR CONGRESS
Maryland District Six

P.O. Box 3263
Gaithersburg, Maryland 20878
(301) 963-8261

Direct Democracy:
– LET THE **PEOPLE** DECIDE –

"On every major issue, I shall poll my constituents and vote in Congress strictly as instructed by the majority."

"On every major issue, I shall poll my constituents and vote in Congress strictly as instructed by the majority."

<u>Major Issues:</u> I shall conduct fair and statistically reliable district-wide polls and hold the result binding for my vote in Congress.

<u>Major Issues:</u> At the beginning of Congressional sessions, I shall poll the district's constituency for guidelines, then with my best judgement, vote accordingly. However, even on minor issues, if 1,000 or more constituents so request, I shall conduct a district-wide binding poll.

<u>New Legislation:</u> I will exercise leadership by proposing new legislation in District 6's interest. However, I shall submit new legislation to Congress only if approved by a District-wide poll. Also, if 1,000 or more constituents request new legislation, I shall draft such legislation, submit it to a District-wide poll, and if approved, to Congress.

189

Only a candidate pledged to direct democracy can guarantee that District 6's vote in Congress will <u>reflect not lobbyist, PACs, campaign donors, not even the representative's personal views</u> - but, in the true spirit of democracy, the <u>majority of the District's Voters.</u>

<u>MAKE HISTORY</u> - VOLUNTEER FOR THE NATION'S FIRST DIRECT DEMOCRACY CAMPAIGN

AUTHORIZED BY THE H.D.MAUTNER FOR CONGRESS COMMITTEE

Let District Six Lead the Nation - Volunteer or Contribute Now

The First Direct Democracy Campaign

Text of the Handout given to the Public to introduce them to the ideas of Direct Democracy

---

How Does Direct Democracy Work? Every representative, senator or president dedicated to Direct Democracy votes in Congress or acts as chief executive strictly as directed by the majority of his/her constituents. The majority view is decided by referendums or statistically honest polls. Direct Democracy representatives will poll the constituents as to which issues should be subject to referendums; what are the voters guidelines on minor issues; what new legislation do the constituents wish to pass. The instructions obtained from the constituents will be binding. Direct Democracy candidates will not accept campaign contributions from any organizations or PACs.

Why Direct Democracy? (1) It is the spirit of democracy that the solid good common sense of the people is the best judge of the public's own interest. In contrast, elected officials are corruptible, especially as the power of campaign contributors, PACs and lobbies in Washington grow. (2) In Direct Democracy every issue is decided independently. In contrast, representative democracy forces unreasonable linkages. In voting for a representative on one issue, the citizen also empowers the representative on other issues and policies which the voter often opposes. Also, representatives chosen for personal charisma are often incompetent or objectionable on many issues. In Direct Democracy every issue is judged separately on its own merits; and issues count, not personalities.

Why Now? The founding fathers had to institute the representative system because communications from remote constituents were inefficient. Today, communications are instant, reliable polling methods exist, and computers help to organize the data.

How do we achieve Direct Democracy? We can achieve Direct Democracy without changing the present system in any way, by electing candidates pledged to the Direct Democracy process. As the number of Direct Democracy representatives and senators grows so will the true representation of the public in Congress.

The Long View Ultimately a system of governance by direct popular referenda and polls may develop through constitutional amendments. Such complete Direct Democracy may be practiced from town to global scale.

The Direct Democracy Campaign The American Constitution does not provide for political parties. The Direct Democracy Campaign is an assembly of individuals who wish to exercise true self-government. The Campaign will encourage candidates as individuals pledged to the Direct Democracy procedures. We shall help each other by advice, a network of volunteers for candidates, and possibly by small individual campaign contributions.

What to Do? Join the Direct Democracy Campaign. Volunteer for a Direct Democracy congressional campaign in your area. If there is none, run for office as a candidate pledged to operate follow Direct Democracy principles and procedures.

Reprinted from the Montgomery Journal,
Wednesday, September 12 1984.
Montgomery County Maryland, U. S. A.

Candidate vows to vote popular voice

By CYNTHIA DURCANIN
Journal staff writer

Unlike most politicians who use their stance on issues to get votes, one Democratic write-in candidate for Congress from Gaithersburg wants to be elected on her impartiality to the issues.

Helene Mautner is trying to oust incumbent Democrat Beverly Byron to represent Maryland's 6th District, which includes the northwestern half of Montgomery County and Western Maryland.

She's running under a platform she coined "direct democracy."

Under "direct democracy," Mautner said, her vote would represent that of the majority and not her own opinion. "Although I have strong personal convictions, I will not take a stance on the issues," she said.

"A representative should vote according to the beliefs of his constituency and not in the best interest of his political career."

"What Congress votes for does not always represent the people. I would vote in favor of the majority even if I personally disagreed with their position."

The underlying philosophy of Mautner's campaign is that as an elected official she would give up her personal power to return it to the people, she said.

Mautner, who filed last February with the Frederick County Board of Elections Supervisors, only got 1,700 of the 15,000 signatures needed to be put on the Nov. 6 ballot and decided to run as a write-in candidate.

According to the candidate, today's representative government is too affected by special interest groups and political action committees. "Political action committees support only those politicians who will vote in their best interest," she said.

Mautner, 38, said she called several special interest groups to solicit campaign funds but was refused money because she would not promise to vote favorably on their issues. The candidate said she has spent about $300 out of her own pocket toward her campaign.

She said she thinks her solid education and involvement with presidential and senatorial campaigns qualifies her for a seat in the House.

"Direct democracy" is nothing new — it's simply an individual promising to vote according to what the district believes is best for them, she said. By refusing to accept funds from special interest groups, she is not obligated to any money interests, she said.

Appendix 3
Organizations, Activities and Books

Organizations

The following list of organizations and internet sites was current at the time of publication. Because of the fluctuating nature of websites on the internet, some of these sites might no longer be operating.

Australia
- Australian Direct Democracy Forum (www.ao.com.au) Scroll down to "Direct Democracy".
- Citizens Initiated Referendums (http://plato.itsc.adfa.edu.au/apr/cir.html)

Bulgaria
- Civic Participation (http//members.tripod.com/~freeinf/)

Canada:
- Canadians for Direct Democracy (CDD) - A Referendum Advocacy Group,
- Vancouver (www.npsnet.com/cdd/indexa.htm)
- Participatory Direct Democracy Association (www.pangea.ca/~sage2509/direct-democracy/)
- Participatory Direct Democracy Association of Winnipeg (www.pangea.ca/~sage2509/direct-democracy/index.html)
- Democracy Watch (www.dwatch.ca/)
- Democracy Science (http://website.lineone.net/~richard.lung)
- Fair Voting BC (www.corp.direct.ca/news/fair.voting.bc/)

Czech Republic:
- Worldwide Direct Democracy (www.phil.muni.cz/~binka/worldwid.html)

Denmark:
- Gotzespace DEMOCR@CY - Conference on Democracy and Internet (www.gotzespace.dk/index.shtml) Germany:

Great Britain
- Direct Democracy Campaign UK (www.homeusers.prestel.co.uk/rodmell)

India:

- Rahul Mehta: How to start DD
  (www.pangea.ca/kolar/DD/Mehta.html)

Italy:

- Italian CICDD e-mail discussion list
  (www.eGroups.com/group/listadd/)
- The Italian CICDD List: Associazione Democrazia Diretta
  (www.geocities.com/CapitolHill/Senate/3412/ald_ita.htm)

Netherlands:

- Digital Citizens Foundation (www.db.nl/english/index.html)

New Zealand

- Direct Democracy Society - An Internet-based organisation for "Direct Democracy Around the World - Toward a World Direct Democracy". Materials for candidates running as Direct Democracy Representatives in local Councils and national Parliaments, based on the first US Direct Democracy Campaign; proposals for a World Direct Democracy; excerpts from "A Constitution of Direct Democracy". (www.Direct-Democracy-Society.org)

Sweden:

- Interactive Representative Direct Democracy (www.ird.nu)

Switzerland:

- Europa Magazine by Forum für direkte Demokratie - language selection available on website. (http://europa.crossnet.ch/)
- University of Geneva Centre on Direct Democracy (http://c2d.unige.ch/)
- Swiss national ballots (www.admin.ch/ch/d/pore/va/list.html)

United States:

- Committee for Direct Democracy (www.dawnpisturino.com)
- Direct Democracy Center (www.realdemocracy.com)
- Initiative and Referendum Institute (www.iandrinstitute.org)
- National Voter Outreach (www.directdemocracy.com)
- Teledemocracy Action News + Network - TAN+N2 Auburn University. Website of the Global Democracy Movement in the USA. (www.auburn.edu/tann)
- Democracies Online Newswire (www.e-democracy.org/do/)
- Direct Democracy League (www.mindspring.com/~sneitzke/)
- Olympians Concerned About Democracy seeking phone voting for Olympia, WA (www.olywa.net/ocad)
- The Pollite Lens (www.pollite.org/site/main/welcome.html)
- Citizens Jury® projects by Jefferson Center (www.jefferson-center.org/)
- New Democracy (www.mich.com/~donald/first.html)
- Approaching Democracy Online (http://democracy.ucdavis.edu/)

- None of The Above - a useful improvement of representative democracy (currently just a title page - no information) (www.nader96.org/bnota.htm)
- U.S. Deliberative Democracy (http://darkwing.uoregon.edu/~ddp/)
- Philadelphia II (www.vote.org/v/index.html)
- Democracy and Internet Workgroup (www.sas.upenn.edu/~eumansky/net.dem.html)

The World:

- Continuing International Congress on DD (CICDD) e-mail discussion list (www.egroups.com/group/cicdd/)

Activities and Conferences

The Continuing International Congress on Direct Democracy

The first International Congress on Direct Democracy was held in Pribram, a suburb of Prague in the Czech Republic on August 25-27 1998.

The second International Congress on Direct Democracy is scheduled to take place in Athens and Delphi Greece, June 21-25 2000.

Books

The following is a sample list of books and other publications dealing with the subject of Direct Democracy. This list was assembled from various sources and the authors of this book cannot verify the accuracy of all the details.

Citizens as Legislators: Direct Democracy in the United States, Shaun Bowler (Editor), Todd Donovan (Editor), Samuel C. Patterson, Ohio State University Press, August 1998

Demanding Choices: Opinion, Voting, and Direct Democracy, Shaun Bowler, Todd Donovan University of Michigan Press, January 1999

Direct Democracy : The Politics of Initiative, Referendum and Recall, Thomas E. Cronin, Replica Books, February 2000

Direct Democracy and International Politics: Deciding International Issues through Referendums, John T. Rourke, Richard P. Hiskes, Cyrus Ernesto Zirakzadeh, Lynne Rienner, Publishers, Inc., January 1992

Direct Democracy in Canada, Patrick Boyer, Published 1992

Direct Democracy in South Dakota: The People Conducting Their Own Business, C. Kenneth Meyer, University of South Dakota, Governmental Research Bureau, January 1979

Direct Democracy: The Politics of Initiative, Referendum, and Recall, Thomas E. Cronin, M. J. Rossant, Published 1999

Instruments of Direct Democracy in the Member States of the Council of Europe, Council of Europe Publishing (Editor), Manhattan, January 1996

Politics of Direct Democracy in the 1980's (Institute for Government and

Politics), McGuigan, Published 1985

Polling and the Democratic Consensus, L. John Martin, in The Annals of the American Academy of Political and Social Science, vlume 472, Sage Publications, Beverly Hills, California 1984

Public Opinion Polls and Democacy, Irving Crespi, Westview Press, Boulder, Colorado 1989.

Referendum: Direct Democracy in Switzerland, Kris William Kobach, Ashgate Publishing Company, January 1993

Referendums around the World: The Growing Use of Direct Democracy, David Butler (Editor),Austin Ranney (Editor), American Enterprise Institute for Public Policy Research, August 1994

Referendums around the World: The Growing Use of Direct Democracy, David Butler, With Austin Rammey, American Entrepreneurs Association, August 1994

Report on the New Zealand Televote, Conducted for the Commission on the Future. Theodor L. Becker. Published by The Commission on the Future, Wellington, 1981.

Representation Versus Direct Democracy in Fighting about Taxes: Conflicting Notions of Sovereignty, Legitimacy, and Civility in Relation to a Tax Fight, Lewis Anthony Dexter, Transaction, December 1982

Tax Crusaders and the Politics of Direct Democracy, Daniel A. Smith, Routledge, August 1998

The Challenge of Direct Democracy: The 1992 Canadian Referendum, Richard Johnston, Neil Nevitte, Andre Blais, Elisabeth Gidengil, McGill-Queens, University Press, October 1996

The New Challenge of Direct Democracy, Ian Budge, Polity Press, January 1997

The Referendum : Direct Democracy in Switzerland, Kris W. Kobach, Published 1993

The Voice of the People: Public Opinion and Democracy. James S. Fishkin, Yale University Press, New Haven, 1995

Un-vote for a New America: A Giude for Constitutional Revolution. Theodor L. Becker, Allyn and Bacon, Boston, 1976.

What American Really Think: and Why Our Politicians Pay No Attention. Barry Sussman, Pantheon Books, New York, 1988.

Appendix 4
The Public Wisdom: Applying Azuma's Inequality

We want to calculate the probability of a majority of right votes ("a" votes) out of n votes cast in a referendum. Statistics often uses reverse arguments. We want to calculate the probability P of an outcome of x wrong votes ("b" votes) out of n votes cast; the rest of the votes, (n - x votes) are right votes. As we argued above, we assume that the probability that an even marginally intelligent voter will make the right decision is better than a 50% random chance. Then the probability of a wrong "b" vote by any individual voter is less than 50%, ie., the probability θ is less than 0.5. We can now use Azuma's inequality
$P(x - n\theta \geq \lambda) \leq \exp(-\lambda^2/2n)$.

The term $x - n\theta$ in the parentheses gives the number by which the actual x wrong "b" votes exceed $n\theta$ which is the statistical number of expected wrong votes. For example, if $\theta = 0.4$ and $n = 100$, then $n\theta = 40$ is the expected number of "b" votes out of 100 votes. Of course, with 100 votes, the number of wrong votes x needs to be more than 50 for a wrong majority decision. In general, x needs to be more than half of the votes, that is, $> n/2$ for a majority of wrong votes. Then it is necessary that $(x - n\theta) > (n/2 - n\theta)$ for a majority wrong vote, ie, $\lambda = n/2 - n\theta$ is substituted into Azuma's inequality. The inequality then gives $P_b \leq \exp(-n(0.5 - \theta)^2/2)$ for the probability P_b of a majority "wrong" vote and correspondingly, $P_a > (1 - \exp(-n(0.5 - \theta)^2/2))$ for the probability P_a of a majority "right" vote.

Of course, this is a simple model with absolute "right" or "wrong" decisions. More complex models are needed if each decision can be fractionally "right" or "wrong" and if there a distribution of probabilities that various people will vote right or wrong. Nevertheless, the results illustrate the main trend, that the probability of a right majority decision increases with the chance $(1 - \theta)$ that any individual makes a right decision and also increases with the number n of voters.

The following Table shows that probabilities of a majority "right" decision as a function of individual wisdom as defined by $(1 - \theta)$ and as a function of n, the number of voters. These probabilities can be compared with the probabilities of right decision by a government. For example, the Table shows that even with marginally intelligent "51%

wise" voters, a referendum by 50,000 voters have a better chance to make the right majority decision than an excellent "90% wise" government. With modestly intelligent "60% wise" voters, a poll of as few as 500 voters will have a better chance to make the right decision than an excellent government. The results are also presented in the form of a graph.

Glossary

Amendment Referendums

> An amendment to amend the Constitution. They must be requested by public proposals submitted by two percent of the voters for two consecutive years, or by eighty percent of the Executive Council for four consecutive years.
>
> Amendment Referendums will be debated during a National Referendum.

Budget Referendum

> Budget Referendums decide the major divisions of the budget on a "pie chart" basis, proportioning the budget among major spending categories

Ceremonial Committee

> A Ceremonial Committee of three citizens (and an alternate) is chosen by lot for a six-month term and is instructed in protocol. They represent the public in ceremonies, sign international treaties, receive foreign dignitaries, distribute awards and in general represent the State at ceremonial occasions.

Debate Period

> The two-months immediately preceding the referendum.

Debates Agency

> Debates Agency has the responsibility of organizing and conducting informed debates and referendum issues.

Election Agency

> The Election Agency selects eight preliminary candidates for each public office, by lot, from the list of qualified and willing candidates.

Election Panels

> The Election Panels narrow down the list of candidates for public office.

Emergency Poll

> If 50,000 voters request an issue within a two-month period it will be subject to an Emergency Poll.

Emergency Referendum

> When 100,000 voters request a proposal issue within any two-month period it will immediately be subject to an Emergency Referendum.

Executive Ombudsman

> The Executive Ombudsman handles urgent emergencies that require immediate responses until the Executive Council can convene. The Executive Ombudsman also chairs the proceedings of the Executive Council, but has no other powers.

Expert Agencies

> Expert Agencies are responsible for carrying out the decisions and policies made by the public through referendums and polls.

Head of the Expert Agency

> A publicly elected head of an Expert Agency for one term of ten years.

Glossary

The Head of an Expert Agency will need to possess at least ten years of experience in the area of expertise of the Agency, including five years of experience in management.

Homo Spaciense and Homo Spascience

Homo Sapiens that are born of space and science.

Human adaptation to space through designed evolution, giving rise to space-adapted life forms. Homo Sapiens will transform themselves into Homo Spaciense, (or, being adapted to space through science, into "Homo Spasciense").

Initiatives

Same as Proposals

Issue Panels

- The Debates Agency forms an Issue Panel for each referendum issue. The Panel is comprised of experts who are advocates for each of the policy issue alternatives, as well as independent members selected randomly from the public.

- Issue Panels receive a list of the policy issue alternatives from the National Proposal Bank and then re-defines each of the issues and prepares the arguments for and against each policy alternatives.

- Issue Panels prepare the information material about the issues for the debates and ensures that the information reaches the public.

List of Proposals

The National Proposal Bank receives submissions from the public and creates a list of proposals, which is then given to the Issue Panel for review and rewording.

National Proposal Bank

The National Proposal Bank collects and counts the proposals that were submitted by the public. These proposals make up the referendum and poll issues that are later put to the public for a vote.

PACs

Political Action Committees. These committees are set up as a loophole to avoid the monetary limitations set by the United States Government to control contributions to political campaigns. The law limits the amount of contributions permitted to political parties by individuals and organizations. However, contributions to Political Action Committees (PACs) do not have to follow the same rules because they are not a political party and therefore, large sums of money are passed through the PACs and eventually become part of the greater campaign fund.

Policy Jury

A Policy Jury is attached to each Expert Agency. They are responsible for examining the actions of the Expert Agency and ensuring that they comply with the public law.

Poll Jury

>Poll Juries review the material that was prepared by the Issue Panels before it is distributed to the poll respondents to ensure that the material is balanced and not manipulative.

Poll Respondents

>The voting for each poll is done by a group of poll respondents who were randomly selected from the public. The number of respondents must be large enough to represent the overall voting public. For example, there may be 2,000 respondents for each poll.

Polls Preferential Voting System

>When there are three or more issue options to choose from in a poll, a polls preferential voting system is used to select the preferred option. Poll respondents vote by ranking each option as either their first, second or third choice. Respondents may also select to vote for only one or two of the options. In scoring, each first vote received 3 points, each second vote receives 2 points and each third vote receives 1 point. The option selected is the one with the highest-ranking scores.

Polls

>When issues of policy are presented to a group of Poll Respondents for a vote.

>Polls are similar to referendums except whereas the entire voting population votes in a referendum, a poll is voted on by thousands of Poll Respondents, who represent a statistically accurate cross-section of the general public. Poll Respondents receive more detailed education about the issue than it is possible to communicate to the general public.

Pre-referendum Screening Poll

>When there are three or more issue options for a referendum, a pre-referendum screening poll is used to reduce the number of options to two. Having only two issue options ensures that a majority decision can be made.

Proposal Bank Jury

>The Proposal Bank Jury examines the groupings and tallies of the proposals that were submitted by the public and prepared by the National Proposal Bank.

Proposal Period

>The period between January through July when the public submits proposals to the National Proposal Bank.

Public Agenda

>The list of referendum and poll issues that are presented to the public for voting during the annual National Referendum and Poll period.

Glossary

Public Ombudsman for Debates
>The Public Ombudsman for Debates carefully reviews the wording of the issue options, prepared by the Issue Panels, to confirm that they are indeed consistent with the spirit of the original proposals received from the public.

Public Ombudsman
>The public elects the Public Ombudsmen in a general election.
>
>One Public Ombudsman is adjunct to each Expert Agency. The Public Ombudsman will assure that the execution of policy reflects the public will.

Referendum Jury
>The Referendum Jury makes sure that the final policy options decided by the Issue Panel correctly represents the content of the public proposals. The Referendum Jury also ensures that the arguments for the public debate are factual and not manipulative.

Referendum and Poll Agency
>The Referendum and Poll Agency manages the conduct of referendums and polls. It ensures the orderly conduct of referendums and polls and the accurate tallying of the votes.

Referendum
>When issues of policy are presented to the public for a general vote. The decisions of referendum in a Direct Democracy system are binding and become the law.

Representative of State
>These are members of the public who are randomly selected to serve as ceremonial hosts. Representatives of State will fulfil all the functions ordinarily performed by state dignitaries.

The Supreme Court
>The Supreme Court is composed of the Chief Justices of the Expert Courts. Members of the Supreme Court are elected publicly. Decisions of the Expert Courts can be appealed to the Supreme Court.

Voters Forums
>Groups of voters nationwide, who are interested in a specialized policy area and become educated in that field. All of these interested and educated citizens are then polled on the main issues in that area.

World Government Organization
>A global system of Direct Democracy. The World Government Organization would manage those affairs that are international, that extend across borders or that have clear implications for the whole human community.

Biographical Note

This work emerged from the need for the common human wisdom when facing a future that will transform the human species. These developments are coming fast and with great promise. However, we also face the warnings of recent history, a holocaust caused by the absence of democracy and the threats of nuclear disaster caused by the shortcomings of representative democracy. Against these prospects and warnings we realize that most people desire peace, prosperity and human survival. This shared wisdom is our best guide toward a grand and secure future.

Michael Noah Mautner was born in Budapest, Hungary in 1942 during the Holocaust. When democracy was swept aside, a war exterminated innocent millions who would have wanted only peace and security. The author lost his father and over sixty relatives, and was saved only by the heroism of a Hungarian women, and acts of humane compassion against the darkest of evil. After World War II, the author grew up under Stalinist dictatorship that substituted a social theory over common sense, and caused further mass suffering. Subsequently, he enjoyed various forms of democracy in Israel, the US and New Zealand. While vastly superior to dictatorship, all of these democracies nevertheless often pursued policies opposite to the wishes of the majority.

In particular, the author and his wife were appalled by the nuclear arms race that built up, against the wishes of most people, arsenals of overkill that threatened his family, billions of lives around the world and indeed, human existence itself. This threat is still with us and is now joined by potential threats of human genetic mis-engineering and possibly robot takeover. These developments can alter or threaten our shared future, yet they are pursued without consulting the majority of the people.

Motivated by these concerns, we started to design a system by which the shared desire for survival, peace and justice of the great majority can turn into the ultimate tools of governance. Some of these ideas were tested out on a modest scale when Helene D. Mautner ran a model local campaign as a Direct Democracy Representative for the United States Congress, as means allowed, and found thousands of people, even in a small local area, supportive of Direct Democracy.

The author obtained a B. Sc. degree in chemistry in the Hebrew University, Jerusalem. He obtained a Ph. D. degree in Physical

Chemistry at The Rockefeller University in New York and served there as Assistant and Associate Professor, followed by appointments as a Research Chemist at the National Institute of Standards and Technology, Research Professor at the Virginia Commonwealth University and Senior Fellow at the University of Canterbury and Lincoln University in New Zealand. He is the author of over 140 research papers and book chapters on ion chemistry, astrochemistry and astrobiology, and is a contributor of articles to the "Futurist" on science, society and the human future. He is a founder/coordinator of the Society for the Expansion of Life in Space.

Together with his wife Helene who edited this book, the author participated as a grass roots activist in the Nuclear Freeze Movement in the U.S. and as grass roots environmental and political campaign activists in the U.S. and in New Zealand.

The author experienced democracy and totalitarianism, and the extremes of good and evil, genius and folly. He shared ideas with people from diverse cultures and is involved actively in the progress that is transforming humankind. From these diverse experiences of life, science and society emerges his conviction that we must be governed by the common wisdom of Life rooted in human nature, which reflects in the common will of the human family. Governed by this shared wisdom, we can fulfil a great human destiny.

~ Part VIII Appendix

www.ingramcontent.com/pod-product-compliance
Lightning Source LLC
Chambersburg PA
CBHW031156270326
41931CB00006B/294